OFF THE LOOM

Creating with fibre

Shirley Marein

Studio Vista London

This book is dedicated to Edmund Marein whose absolute
confidence in the abilities of others creates confidence.

*TT848
.M37
1972b

© Shirley Marein 1972
Designer. Marie-Louise Luxemburg
Editor. Erica Hunningher
First published in Great Britain 1972 by
Studio Vista, Blue Star House, Highgate Hill,
London N19

Set in 11pt Plantin 110
Photoset and printed in Great Britain by BAS Printers Limited,
Wallop, Hampshire

Bound by Webb, Son & Co., Southgate, London

ISBN 0 289 70254 2

Contents

1 How it started

To many people weaving is associated only with utilitarian needs—baskets to store food, fabrics for warmth and protection—but there is far more to fabric construction than function. Otherwise we would probably find animal skins and bark cloth quite serviceable, as they still are among primitive peoples. Long, long ago man found aesthetic expression almost as necessary to his well-being as the elementary comforts.

The history of textiles, in both the structuring and the designing of fabrics has developed consistently with other cultural accomplishments. There will always be academic dispute between weavers and potters as to who filled the need, somewhere near a river bed, for a container suitable for the first harvest. Some early pottery fragments have an impressed design much like a basket weave and there is speculation that clay was used around baskets in order to make them watertight. Most likely weaving originated in the Mesopotamia area earlier than 5000 BC and spread from this centre to other parts of Europe and Asia. But spindles and whorls, essential for the spinning of thread, have been found all over the world and it may be that weaving developed independently in various areas.

There is knowledge of decorated weaves from the Sumarian cities of the Mediterranean basin, dating from 2900 BC. Excavations on the island of Crete have revealed wall-paintings indicating the Minoan use of tapestry murals. Literature tells of Homer's Helen executing an elaborate scene in two colours and of Penelope working on a wall-hanging while Ulysses was away on a voyage to Troy. Although the Greeks had fine fabrics, there are no early Greek wall-hangings in existence today.

Again, from the Bible comes the quotation 'swifter than the weaver's shuttle' and Joseph had 'a coat of many colours' (probably appliqué stitchery rather than weaving) but the earliest sample fragments date from the time of the Copts, many centuries later.

The most influential and strikingly creative period in the history of weaving occurred in the early centuries of the Christian era. Decorative weaving flowered simultaneously in Egypt, Europe and on the American continent. During the Roman era Hellenic and eastern culture spread through

Fig. 1 Tapestry woven Coptic textile. Decorative panel of linen and wool in brick red, blue and white with warm tan areas. Third or fourth century. Typical Hellenic roundels within squares with a centre portrait of a young man in a hunting tunic. Collection Mr and Mrs Leon Pomerance, New York

Fig. 2 Late Peruvian textile border in reds, yellows and mauve-grey alpaca wool. Decorative water birds executed in outlined interlocked tapestry weave with open slits and warp wrapped detail.
Collection the author

Egypt, having a particularly strong influence on the Copts, a small sect converted to Christianity. A great many fragments of tapestry are preserved from their burial grounds and archaeologists have unearthed fabrics of linen, wool and silk.

The silk worm was brought to the west in about AD 560. Aristotle had described the special quality of silken thread and the Greeks and Romans had purchased silks from merchants travelling the trade routes from the east. No Coptic looms have been discovered as yet. The weaving must have been done on warp-weighted upright looms very similar to those seen on Grecian vases. Often Hellenic geometric motifs were used within roundels, or multiple roundels within squares and meticulous attention was paid to detail in portraits. Scenes from the Bible, designs of fauns and satyrs, vines, fruit and flowers were much used. In about AD 300 the Romans began sending Coptic weavers to Gaul to teach weaving and establish textile centres throughout the northern empire.

At the same time there was another important influence—the Norsemen. Their origins are vague but anthropologists believe that they are most likely to have been in the Iranian racial tradition and that they drifted north from above the Black sea area, a section of present day Soviet Russia. They were a vigorous, vital and very militant group: barbarians, sailors, agriculturalists. By the tenth century they were in possession of the territory in northern France near Rouen and Bayeux, and in other areas even further north. One of the most remarkable wall-hangings, preserved intact from the eleventh century, is known as the Bayeux tapestry. It is

Fig. 3 Spanish satin brocade in yellow, green, salmon, light orange, brown and natural beige silk. Seventeenth century.
Collection the author

8

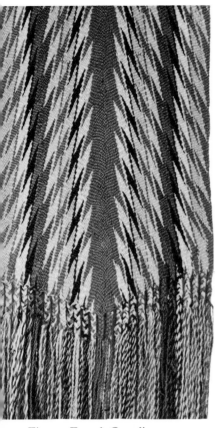

Fig. 4 French Canadian Assomption sash sometimes called *ceinture fléchée* (arrow sash) or *ceinture à flamme* (flame-like). Sashes are eight to nine inches wide with fourteen arrows or points to a foot and may be over fifteen feet long. The fringes were braided for two inches; then several strands were twisted together until plyed, ending with a knot and a tuft.
Collection Cooper-Hewitt Museum of Design, Smithsonian Institution, New York

remarkable because of its size, two hundred and thirty feet long by twenty inches in height; it is remarkable because of its subject matter, William Duke of Normandy slaying Earl Harold in the Battle of Hastings and thereby securing the Norman conquest of England; and it is remarkable because it is embroidered on a woven background at a time when needles were made of bone, wood or ivory. The steel needle was not invented until the sixteenth century. Norse burial ships, sunk and preserved in the sands below the water, have revealed tapestry fragments representing many types of figures and varieties of trees. The twelfth-century Baldishol tapestry of Hedmark, Norway, represented the months of the year, a favourite theme since the classical period.

Weaving flourished in the western hemisphere, notably in Peru where the arid coastal burial grounds preserved the most amazing textiles, including intricate embroideries, complicated weaves, tapestries and also single element fabrics: netting, knitting, braiding, plaiting and knotting. Cloth several yards wide has been found wrapped around the dead, indicating understanding of the sophisticated intricacies of weaving on warps arranged in multiple layers. Pre-Incan and Incan tapestries incorporate every known fabric structuring, except perhaps the knotting of the Persian rug makers. Weaving spread north from Central America to Mexico to what is now the United States, diminishing in virtuosity along the way, possibly because of a lack of ready materials. Peruvian coastal areas produced cotton and the mountains abounded with vicuna, llama and alpaca. The Indians of North America were versatile in their usage of twining. Twining developed from a functional need for storage pouches, baskets and carrying aids. The art of twining achieved unusual distinction in the ceremonial weaving of the Chilkat Indians of the North Pacific Coast.

The Romans had established the first weaving centres in France, from Arles to Arras. When the Pope moved to Avignon the Italian influence became even more widespread and the luxury fabrics of France, Spain and Italy were hardly distinguishable.

Art is significant as a personal expression, although much that has survived has lost its original social and religious meaning. The tapestries of the French medieval weavers, as protection against cold, were as essential to comfort as were the religiously satisfying prayer rugs to the Moslems. In medieval castles wall paintings faded and peeled in damp northern climates. Tapestries and embroidered hangings were more permanent and contributed warmth to the huge draughty rooms as well as stilling the echoes that resounded from stone floors and walls. They had the further advantage of being portable, for the landowners moved from castle to castle with all their possessions. From a social point of view

9

Fig. 5   Oriental rug of wool and
silk with a gold metallic thread
in tapestry woven areas; wild
animals, lions, spotted cats and
deer with antlers against a floral
ground.
Collection Norma Kershaw,
New York; Photo Curt Meinel

Fig. 6   Brussels tapestry
representing the goddess Flora,
c. 1580.
Collection the author

it is interesting to note that in 1292 there were twenty-four
tapestry makers in Paris but two centuries later the town of
Arras, a little to the north of Paris, employed 14,000 weavers.

During the reign of Louis XIV the French tapestry
weavers were united and the Gobelin factory was founded
in Paris. Because of oppression many fled and inadvertently
France was instrumental in spreading her weaving knowledge
and skills to other lands. Some went to Flanders and still
others, the Huguenots, to England and North America.

In North America the eastern Indians were intrigued and
excited by the finery of the French Canadian fur traders,
who carefully set the stage for fur trading and barter by
impressing them with their superiority, displaying lavish
personal adornment. Their greatcoats were held together
with magnificent wide braided sashes of strong bright colours
having long fringes and tufted tips. Bright red cloth leggings
were secured at the knee and upper thigh with garters braided
in the chevron pattern and wrapped round and round. The
desire to emulate, to acquire, and to be as impressive, started
a widespread diffusion of European trade items and the home
manufacture of these handicrafts.

2 Fingers are tools

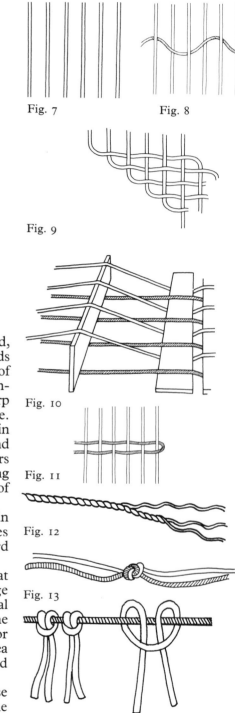

Fig. 7   Fig. 8

Fig. 9

Fig. 10

Fig. 11

Fig. 12

Fig. 13

Fig. 14 Reverse double half hitch

Warp parallel threads running lengthwise (fig. 7).

Weft supplementary thread woven over and under warp threads (fig. 8).

Self weft each warp thread assumes the function of a weft thread, then returns to its warp position (fig. 9).

Shed opening formed when alternate threads are lifted (fig. 10).

Plain weave (also called tabby) alternate over and under interlacing, or the placing of each row of weft in an open shed (fig. 11).

Ply threads or yarns twisted together (fig. 12).

Overhand knot form a loop, bring one end through opening in loop, pull ends to tighten (fig. 13).

Braiding is a simple way to begin. Think of a simple braid, as one would braid a child's hair: three parallel strands running lengthwise, the end strand assuming the function of the weft; weave alternately over and under the others including the last strand; return the last strand to vertical warp position. Always start with the end strand from same side.

Multicoloured strands in even units are very effective in braiding. Start with four red strands, four white strands and four blue strands. Any group of strong contrasting colours will aid in understanding the structure as the weaving proceeds. Use 2-ply or heavier rug yarn cut in lengths of two yards each. There are several ways to start.

For a belt with a buckle, fold two four-yard lengths in half, attach to the buckle with reverse double half hitches (fig. 14) (a basic macramé knot) making four two-yard lengths of each colour.

A wrap around belt with a fringe (fig. 15) will require at least an extra foot of warp yarn added to the length. Arrange the lengths according to colour scheme, try a symmetrical layout. Tie an overhand knot in the top six inches of the group. Loop each length once around the top of a pencil or dowel; keep all warp lengths on the same side. The area reserved for the fringe may be held together with an overhand knot (fig. 16).

A wall-hanging can be started with as many reverse double half hitches over a holding rod as necessary for the desired width.

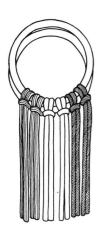

Fig. 15   Reverse double half
hitches attached to a double ring
belt buckle

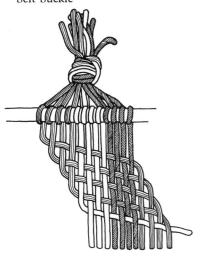

Fig. 16   Braiding in three colours,
looped around a dowel

Fig. 17   Braiding worked in the
French Canadian manner—
pinned to the crossed knee

Fig. 18   Three-colour braiding: on
the left, loosely woven with an
open warp and weft; in the
centre, the weft is covered and
the weaving diagonal from the
left; on the right, each group
of colours is braided as a single
unit

Support the top of the warp in the most comfortable way.
Attach it to a door knob, the back of a chair or to a nail in
the door jamb. A good method is to put the top part in a
waist-high dresser drawer, close the drawer gently to hold
the work and pull up a chair. The nineteenth-century
French Canadian method of pinning a narrow piece of work
to the crossed knee is very effective (fig. 17).

Loosely woven, the colour of the warp and the weft will
be equally visible. Tighter weaving in which the weft is
completely covered results in a variety of pattern depending
upon the colour combinations of the warp. The warp divided
into three equal colours as suggested will create alternating
diagonal stripes. Variations in the arrangement of the colour
threading account for the basic pattern differences. Braiding
from one side shows a strong diagonal ridge. Change the
direction of the diagonal by starting from the other side.

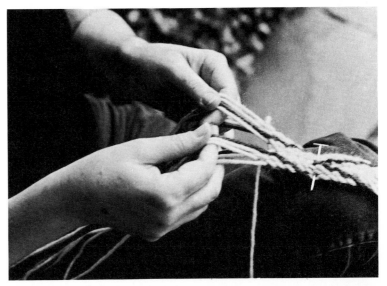

Braiding: self weft finger weaving

Pick up every other thread, moving them on to the top of the index finger. The alternate threads are between the index and the third finger (fig. 19). Now you have an open shed.

Switch the threads held in this position from hand to hand. Become accustomed to holding the yarns in either hand. Never lose the shed. Your index finger is acting as a shed stick. Take the first thread from the left and pull it through the shed.

Change the shed. Pick up the threads that were between the index and the third finger, one at a time, placing the first one over the index finger, alternating and exchanging places with the other threads. When you have worked across the row all the threads will have exchanged positions. The new shed is now open and ready for another weft.

The next warp at the left is pulled through the shed, becoming in effect a weft thread. When it reaches the right-hand side it changes place with the last self weft.

The last self weft resumes a warp position, either over or under the previous thread, in accordance with the weaving structure of alternating one warp over the weft and one warp under the weft.

Fig. 19   Position of the fingers in the open shed

The chevron pattern

The chevron pattern (fig. 20) can be woven in two ways: from the centre to the outside edge and from the outside edge towards the centre. Weaving outwards from the centre, proceed as follows.

Prepare the warp with symmetrical threading. The easiest pattern to weave is with two contrasting colours. The number of warp threads should be divisible by 2 or 3.

Tie the warp threads together and support the top.

Hold the warp threads taut over the fingers of the left hand and pick up every other thread with the right hand. Half the threads will be placed over the index finger and the others between the index and the third finger.

Hold the threads in order across the top of the index fingers. Practise opening the shed. Change threads to the right hand. Do not lose the shed.

Lift the centre right-hand thread from the top group and pass it through the shed to the left. Gently pull it out to the left.

Change all the threads to the left hand and lift the top centre left-hand thread, pass it through the shed and pull it out to the right.

Change the shed. This is done after every shot of weft thread, to lock the weft into place. Start each unit from the same side. With the threads in the right hand, pick up each thread in position under the weft with the index finger and

Fig. 20   Braided chevron pattern

thumb of the left hand, take the next thread, on top of the weft and drop it down between the third and fourth finger of the right hand.

Open the shed. Pull the right-hand centre thread through the shed until it is parallel with the last weft thread pulled out to the left side. Depending on the position of the last vertical warp, place the upper weft thread over or under the current weft and allow the upper thread to join the vertical warp threads.

Plain weave with supplementary weft

Plain weave or tabby is the basic interlacing of vertical and horizontal threads. The weft held at right angles to the warp is worked in finger weaving by attaching an extra, individual weft thread to the top of the group of threads and carrying it alternately over and under successive warp threads from one side to the other. The auxiliary weft must be long enough to complete a good part of the work. When the weft thread is almost used up, allow a four-inch end to drop behind a warp thread near the centre of the work. Start with a new weft thread in the same space, dropping a four-inch end behind the work. Never begin or end at the selvedge. When the piece is concluded the loose ends should be carefully woven or pulled back through the web with a crochet hook and clipped.

Braiding and plaiting with shed sticks
Both braiding and plaiting with shed sticks are very ancient techniques. Both are worked on a taut warp. Constructed at one end, when the shed is opened the construction is automatically duplicated at the other end, eventually meeting in the centre. There is confusion about this form of warp twining because there are so many different terms and names used all over the world: sprang, frame-plaiting, Egyptian

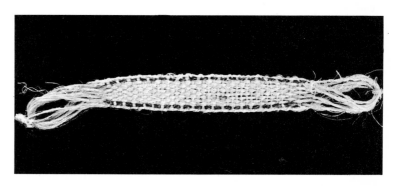

Fig. 21 Mexican tump line in
plain weave with continuous warp

plaitwork, meshwork, twine-plaiting, loom-braiding, knotless netting, Mexican and Swedish braiding. Irene Emery in her book *Primary Structures of Fabrics* defines the differences by noting that braiding is interlacing and plaiting is interlinking. Plaiting is commonly called sprang (derived from *språngning*, of old Swedish origin), meaning the method as well as the structure. Both braiding and sprang are worked with a continuous warp stretched between two adjustable bars so that the tension can be released as necessary. Braiding is interlaced and sprang or meshwork is interlinked with a twist. Both forms have great stretchability. Braiding and sprang have a variety of functional uses—for belts, bags, carryalls, hammocks and other forms requiring open network. Sprang, however, is extremely interesting used decoratively, expanded and held taut at the sides or fashioned in the round supported by circular wires. Sprang can also be used in conjunction with weaving on the loom if consideration is given to releasing the tension.

The terms 1/1, 2/2 and 3/3 braid refer to the number of warp threads interacting with each other. For instance in a 1/1 braid, one warp crosses over another single warp. In a 2/2 braid, two warp strands are used in unison over two other warp threads. The traditional Hopi Indian braided wedding sashes are constructed in a 3/3 braid, with three warp threads raised and crossed and three dropped. The 3/3 braid must be arranged in sequences of three with one extra warp thread. The 1/1 and 2/2 braids may have any number of threads.

In sprang or meshwork the warps are twisted (linked together): 1/1 sprang is one warp interlinked with another single warp thread (fig. 22a) while 2/2 sprang is the same single warp interlinked with another single warp thread twisted around each other twice (fig. 22b). 3/3 sprang is twisted several times making a more open structure and increasing the tension (fig. 22c). Diversions in the warp are arranged by alternating 1/1 twists, 2/2 twists and 3/3 twists. A few points to consider before starting:

1   Stretch the warp tautly between two sticks or dowels, vertically or horizontally.

2   A frame or canvas stretcher are suitable for small pieces. Consider using the Ojibway loom (see fig. 40). Large pieces must be suspended from a height and weighted at the bottom with a bar. Additional weights may be required.

3   If a frame or stretcher is used, hold the sticks in position with heavy rubber bands or suspend sticks from the frame so that they can be tied and untied as necessary to release the tension.

4   Shed sticks are necessary. Slender circular sticks are best. For narrow widths knitting needles or hibachi skewers are handy; longer widths require dowels or thin laths, sanded

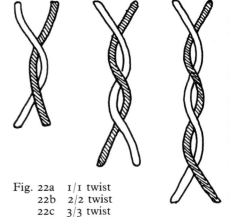

Fig. 22a   1/1 twist
22b   2/2 twist
22c   3/3 twist

and pointed. Seven shed sticks are used, three at one end and four at the opposite end, rotating the fourth stick from side to side with each new row.

5 Check each row to see that no errors have been made. Mistakes are difficult to correct once the shed sticks have been removed. Each time the shed sticks are rotated roll back the stick nearest the beginning and end of the work to tighten the row.

6 At the centre, when it is no longer possible to manipulate the warp, thread a large holed yarn needle with the warp yarn and insert a few rows of plain weave. Experiment with finishes at the centre. It is possible to tie each unit on the back with an invisible thread of cotton or nylon, or to insert a decorative rod through the centre. Without this centre holding the entire work will unravel.

Simple 1/1 braid

Practise on a small piece with an all-over braid. (Braiding and sprang can be mixed on one piece.) Select three colours in order to understand the colour movement: three red, six white, six blue and three red warp ends. Wind the colours, equally distributed, around the sticks attached with cords or rubber bands to the frame or support. Tie one end of the red warp to one of the sticks, carry it over and under the sticks in a figure-of-eight movement. Tie each successive colour to the last colour at the bottom of the bar. End on the stick with the starting tie.

Open a shed on the side nearest you by picking up alternate threads and weaving a few rows of tabby, ending with the last right-hand thread on the bottom. Remember to open each shed all the way up to the top of the warp, weaving top and bottom rows of tabby simultaneously.

Hold the open upper shed over the index finger of the left hand and the lower part of the shed between the index and the third finger.

First row: Roll the first thread on the right-hand side of the left hand to the edge of the index finger, crossing the bottom thread. With the right hand pick up the first thread from the bottom right-hand side. Slide it up over the top of the index finger of the right hand. Drop the first thread at the edge of the left-hand index finger down into the space between the index and third fingers of the right hand. Continue across until all the warp threads are transferred to the right hand. Slip a shed stick into the bottom and top of the warp. Transfer all warp threads to the left hand.

Second row: Keep the first thread on the right-hand side of the left hand to the left. The first bottom warp slides between the index and third finger of the right hand; pick up the second bottom warp and place over the index finger

of the right hand; now allow the first thread in the upper
warp to fall between the index and third finger of the right
hand. Continue across row; insert shed sticks bottom and top.
Transfer all warp threads to the left hand.

Third row : Repeat first row.

Fourth row: Repeat second row.

Continue this sequence until the centre is reached. Finish
as described above.

Sprang

Sprang, meshwork and Egyptian plaiting are almost the
same. Contemporary sprang differs in the freedom of method
and approach. Today it is a technique used for wall-hangings
and rather unusual costuming. Unique in its flexibility,
sprang can expand and contract. Mobility is unusual in construction techniques, so take advantage of the dimensions
possible. Sprang can be worked attached to a supporting
frame, the frame acting as a functional aid or as an integral
part of the total piece. Without a frame for support suspend
the upper bar at a convenient height; the lower bar may be
secured with screw eyes in the floor or baseboard moulding.
A greater length can be handled by securing the bottom bar
to the floor at an angle similar to the hypotenuse of a triangle.
Remember that you work from one end only, towards the
centre. For a stretched flat piece it may be necessary to
attach a slender vertical support to the top and bottom bars.
Shed sticks can be the same width as the warp or the warp
can be worked and held in sections. Although the method of
working is similar to braiding, a piece that is very wide
cannot be held across the fingers; therefore, use the shed
stick to pick up and carry the warp or work with the fingers
in sections and insert the stick as you proceed. The warp
count is determined by the weight of the fibre used and the
width desired.

Working order of sprang
Stretch a practice warp in the same manner as suggested for
braiding. Although multiple colours can be used, wall-
hangings are more monumental in one or two colours,
worked in linen, nylon or cotton cording. Select a heavy
cotton cording for practice. Knot one end around the
bottom dowel, bring over the upper dowel, down and over
the bottom, up and over, down and over—in effect in a
figure-of-eight pattern (fig. 23). Finish at the bottom on the
same bar as the start. Start immediately or space with a few
rows of plain weave, in which case the first thread at the
right will be in the down position or coming from behind
the bar.

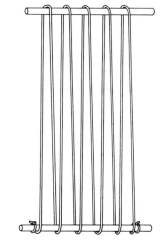

Fig. 23   Sprang warping

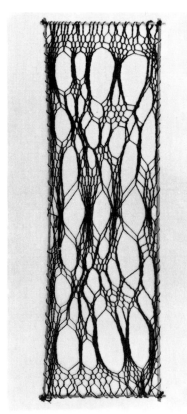

Fig. 24   Sprang by Theresa Dowd
Photo the author

Fig. 25   Wall-hanging by Isolde
Savage. Crocheted in jute

19

20

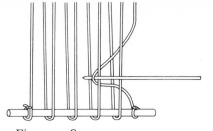

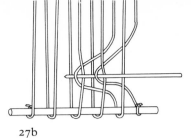

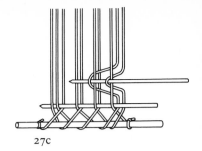

Fig. 27a   Sprang   27b   27c

Fig. 26 *Macrogauze 70* Peter
Collingwood. Black linen with
stainless steel rods, 60 × 41 in.
This is a unique development
from sprang called 'warp
transposing'
Photo Charles Seely

1/1 sprang

First row: Starting on the right, bring cord 1 under cord 2,
over cord 3, under cord 4, then over the right index finger
or a shed stick (fig. 27a). This will twist cords 1 and 4. Then
pick up cord 3, which is untwisted, take it under cord 4
(cord 4 is over the finger or shed stick), over cord 5, under
cord 6 and slip over finger or shed stick (fig. 27b). This will
twist cords 3 and 6. Continue across row. Place shed stick
in first row of 1/1 sprang, place another stick in the same
shed and push it up to the top. If the warp ends are even in
number, there will be two ends under the stick on the right-
hand side and two over the stick on the left.

Second row: Starting on the right, bring cord 1 over cord 2,
under cord 3 and over the right index finger or a shed stick
(fig. 27c). This will twist cords 1 and 3. Then pick up cord 2,
which is untwisted, take it under cord 3 (cord 3 is over the
finger or shed stick), over cord 4 and under cord 5 and slip
over index finger or shed stick. Put another stick in this
shed, then another in the same shed and push up.

Repeat these two rows as a unit so that whenever you
stop working you will know that you must start the first row
again.

2/2 sprang

The procedure is exactly the same as for 1/1 sprang, except
that in the first row cords 1 and 4 are twisted around each
other twice. In the second row cords 1 and 3 are twisted
around each other twice.

3/3 sprang

Again the procedure is exactly the same except that in the
first row cords 1 and 4 are twisted around each other three
times. In the second row cords 1 and 3 are twisted around
each other three times.

Openings in the sprang

Openings for design areas are made by skipping one twist.
For example, if you twist cords 1 and 4 and allow cords 3
and 6 to go untouched, an opening will be started. Place
them above and below the shed stick where they would fall
normally. The opening becomes larger as the skip continues
row after row. Close the opening by crossing the next row
in a straight 1/1, 2/2 or 3/3 twist technique. Finish at the
centre.

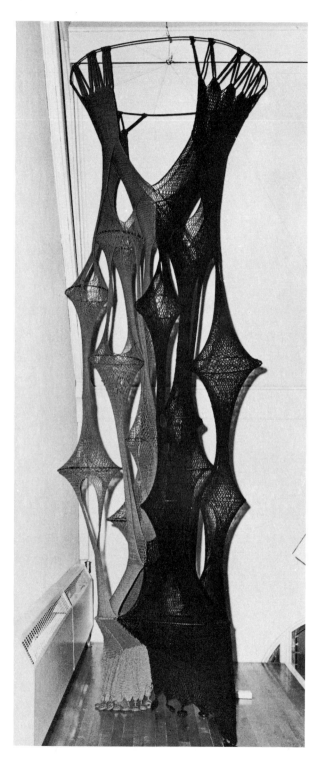

Fig. 28 *Triple Suspension*
May Gower. Bleached hemp with
dark green glass float, 32 in. long.
Tablet weave
Photo Mark Gerson

Fig. 29 *Gemini* Marie Aiken.
Black and purple nylon, 60 ×
180 in. Multilayered sprang,
breaking from a single layer into
sixteen layers
Photo Fry-Gravenhurst, Canada

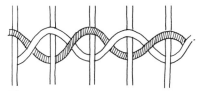

Fig. 30

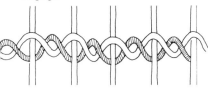

Fig. 31

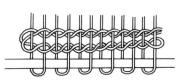

Fig. 32

Fig. 33 Warp attached to loom stick suspended from a frame

Twining

Half turn two wefts crossing over each other between warps (fig. 30).
Full turn two wefts crossing over each other in a complete turn (fig. 31).
Paired turn two wefts crossing over each other, enclosing two warps at a time (fig. 32).

Twining is basic. To twine is to twist around, to entwine, to encircle. It is a method with no specific place of origin, used universally—among the weavers of the far north of the American continent, in Peru, India and among the Maori in remote areas of New Zealand. When a technique works well and needs increase, usage is extended to fit the many different purposes. Twining is essential for holding reeds together and for making baskets. Twining is the way to lace a stockade fence securely, to make mats, to make an open lacy gauze weave, to hold warp threads evenly apart and also to hold warp threads together. To twine is to encircle a warp thread with a doubled over-weft thread. One weft comes from behind the warp, the other across the front, and the two cross each other between warps. Twining can also be the twisting of a warp with no weft. Tablets or tubular beads are occasionally used to help with turning the warp. When the warp changes its vertical position it is called a braided open weave. Weft twining requires no shed, the warp always remains closed. The warp may be rigid, tied down at both ends on a frame, or it may be loose, attached at one end, as on the Ojibway loom. A free-hanging warp is attached to a holding cord with reverse double half hitches. The rigid warp may be attached directly to the loom frame or to a loom stick (a dowel or flat stick suspended from the loom frame). Wind a continuous warp around the loom sticks (fig. 33). Twine across warp; if the weft is very fine, go back and forth several times. Remove from the loom stick; move the twining down to the edge of the warp. Whip the top of the warp to the loom stick. The finished piece will have the effect of four selvedges (figs. 34a and 34b).

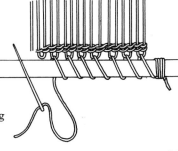

Figs. 34a and 34b Selvedge weaving

Twining is manipulated with the fingers; no shuttles are needed. The long weft ends may be shortened and held in butterflies (fig. 36) or wound round and round the fingers, removed and secured with a rubber band.

The combination of colour is relatively simple. Because the weft must be used double, the front and back halves of the weft may be different colours (fig. 35). A full turn between warp threads of a two-colour weft will bring one

Fig. 35   Two-colour weft tied together with an overhand knot

colour to the front. A half turn between warp threads will alternate the colours. In the *taaniko* weaving of the Maori, many colours are carried across the warp; some are used in the design and others float behind the weaving until needed. Depending on the weaver's technique and the fibre used, the fabric stretches easily. But when many wefts are carried across, the fabric is very firm. If the cord is thick and the overall size large, the wall-hanging or blanket will be heavier than one of comparable size structured in some other technique.

Twining encircles the warp thread in a variety of arrangements:
1   Half turn between warp threads.
2   Half turn between every two warp threads (paired warp).
3   Half turn between one warp thread, then after two warp threads in a 1,2,1,2,1,2 sequence.
4   Full turns.
5   Half turn on paired warp threads; split and alternate pairs every other row (diverted warps).
6   Twining may be compact or spaced between rows, leaving the warp exposed.
In every case one weft passes over the warp or warp threads and the other behind, crossing between the warps, exchanging positions, then proceeding to the next warp or set of warp threads. These variations and the introduction of colour provide many possibilities for distinctive textures and patterns.

At the end of a row, either a plain turn or a countered turn back is possible. Each produces a different effect.

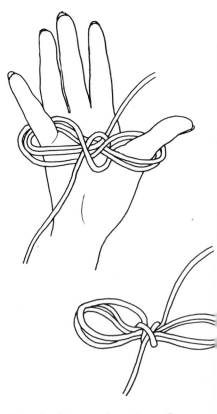

Fig. 36   Constructing a butterfly

Fig. 37   Plain turn

Fig. 38   Countered turn

Fig. 39   Ojibway loom with warp of jute

Fig. 40   Ojibway loom constructed of 2 × 3 in. pine with 1 in. dowels, width 18 in., height 20 in.

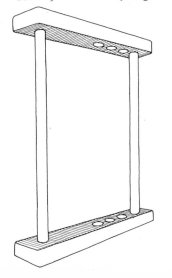

Plain turn

Step one   The weft going over the last warp takes a half turn back, proceeds over the weft emerging from behind the last warp and then goes under the last warp.

Step two   The weft emerging from behind the last warp takes a half turn back, going over the front weft and over the last warp.

Step three   The front weft emerging from behind the last warp after the turn is placed over the second warp and under the third as the twining continues (fig. 37).

Countered turn

Step one   The same as for the plain turn.

Step two   The weft that goes over the warp is pulled towards you. The weft from behind the last warp turns back, over the last warp and under the second warp.

Step three   The weft that is pulled towards you now goes up over the second warp and under the third (fig. 38).

Twining in the round

The Ojibwa, or Chippewa Indians, of the Great Lakes region of the United States, probably designed the prototype for the Ojibway tubular loom (fig. 39). Two stakes driven into the ground, a suitable distance apart, will keep a holding cord taut when wound around the stakes a few times. The warp cords are attached with a reverse double half hitch and the twining worked by moving around the stakes. The Ojibway loom illustrated (fig. 40) is adjustable—the holes top and bottom hold the movable dowels and determine the width of the opening. If the holding cord has a tendency to slip down during the twining, hang it over a small nail inserted in the sides of the dowels or tie the holding cord to the top bar with an auxiliary string. The holding cord could be stapled to the vertical dowel. Turn the loom as you work. The removable top permits a longer piece of tubular weaving. Remove the top, pull up the finished piece, fold it over, pin to the top of the dowels and continue twining.

Dimensional forms may be woven by adding warp cords in reverse double half hitches to the existing warps. The new warp cords may be perpendicular to the existing vertical

25

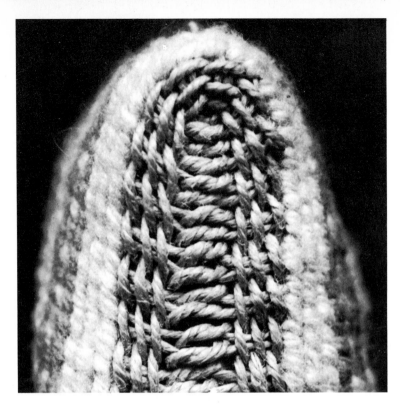

Fig. 41 Pouch bottom (detail) by Diane Milder. The pouch has been drawn together with square knots

Fig. 42 Warp wrapping

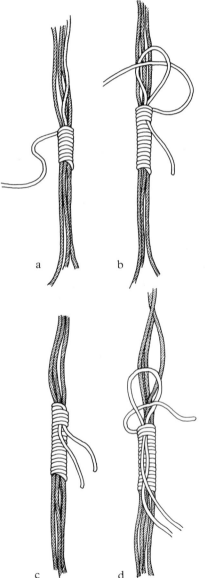

a

b

c

d

warp or they may be added as supplementary cords.

An empty picture frame may be used instead of a loom. Wind the holding cord around the width of the frame to create a rim from which to hang the warp threads.

In order to close one side, necessary for a pouch (fig. 41), work the bottom together with a series of square knots (see macramé, page 33). The width of the square knots should be adjusted so that the sides are joined with ease. With correct tension the sides will come together without buckles and bulges. White or clear glue is helpful in securing any loose ends on the inside.

Warp wrapping

Place a cord of the same or contrasting fibre along the unit to be wrapped and turn tightly over it, from the bottom up or the top down (fig. 42a). When the desired length has been reached double back the end that was placed along the unit; continue winding over it at least five times. Put the working end through the loop that is left (fig. 42b). Pull the end projecting under the last five turns, drawing loops and both ends down through the turns (fig. 42c). Trim.

Alternatively, proceed in the same manner as above but place a shorter cord along the unit to be wrapped. When the desired length is reached place a supplementary cord, doubled over, against the unit and continue winding (fig. 42d). Put the working end through the loop and pull the two

Fig. 43 Pouch by Rhu Mellum.
Yellow and orange wool on jute
with hand-carved beads

projecting ends down, bringing the working end through.
Remove supplementary cord. Trim single end.

Warp twining
A form of warp twining called Hungarian weaving is a fast
and simple technique suited to thick and textured fibres
such as jute and sisal, heavy cotton roving or cable cord.
This type of weaving can, of course, be done on a small scale
using multi-plyed wool, raffia and synthetics. Any number
of household items can be woven, from placemats to door-
mats. Interesting possibilities exist for large forms for wall-
hangings. Consider warp twining combined with macramé
in a sculptural construction. On a large scale malleable wire

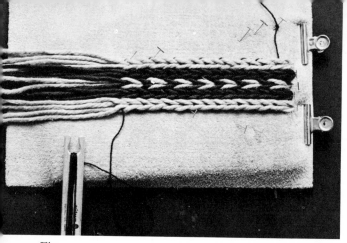

Fig. 44

Fig. 45

added to the weft helps to shape the form. Sections can be attached to each other with a whipped seam, laced together with leather thongs or linked together. A width of five or six inches can be woven on any padded surface (fig. 44) that will hold a T-pin or straight pin (see page 32). But a simple loom made of $\frac{3}{4}$ in. pine, with finishing nails standing upright to space the cords, is handy and easy to make. The illustration (fig. 46) is for an 11×18 in. board with $2\frac{1}{2}$ in. finishing nails arranged $\frac{3}{4}$ in. apart across the top, $1\frac{1}{2}$ in. apart down the sides, with a large 3 in. finishing nail in the last position as an anchor for the weft, alternating from side to side between warp changes.

The warp should be measured and cut twice as long as the finished piece. Each length must be folded in half and looped around the finishing nail at the head of the loom. When a macramé knotting board is used the cords should be secured with pins. If a fringe is desired, tie or make a knot in the top two inches and place over the finishing nails, allowing the ends to extend over the top of the loom. The length of the loop determines the length of the fringe. If the ends are very long, shorten them with a butterfly or wind round the fingers and fasten with a rubber band. Continue across the board covering each nail with a double length of warp.

Now start again with a second colour, putting the second colour over the nails on top of the first row of warp threads. Each nail in the horizontal row at the top of the loom will have two double warp lengths, one on top of the other. With a string, twine across the nails, knot after the last nail and secure the warp lengths.

Weave with the loom on a flat surface. Open the shed by lifting the top row of warp lengths back over the top of the nails at the head of the loom without disturbing the manner in which they are secured. Have in readiness a butterfly of weft composed of either of the colours used. Tie the weft to the nail on the upper left-hand side; leave a generous end

Fig. 44   Warp twining on a macramé knotting board

Fig. 45   The position of the hands for warp twining

Fig. 46   Warp twining board; the twining across the top secures the warps

Fig. 47   Placing the weft

Fig. 48   Warp twining with macramé, in natural and black jute

Fig. 46

Fig. 47

Fig. 48

for weaving back into the top later on. Carry the weft across the shed to the right-hand side (fig. 47), over the first nail on the vertical side and down the outside of the row to the last nail at the bottom end. Loop the weft around this long nail several times to hold it taut. Change the shed by taking down the first set of double threads. With your thumb and index fingers between the top double threads pick up the bottom set and put them over the top of the nails at the top of the loom. Continue across the row. Untie the weft and bring it across the newly opened shed, back to the left and over the second nail, down the outside and secure over the last large nail. Change the sheds by exchanging the positions of the warp. When the end of the board has been reached, undo the twining at the top and carefully pick up the entire piece. Place the loops at the top on a dowel or a holding cord. Move the entire work up to the top of the board and settle it just above the top row of nails. Bring the double warps down into place around the nail heads.

One colour set above another colour will make a pattern of horizontal bars. Alternate a pair of the same colours every other nail for vertical bars. Try a variety of colours in different sequences for pattern effects. The ends can be knotted into a fringe, bound and hemmed, or threaded on a yarn needle and pulled back into the body of the weaving.

The crochet hook and its many uses

Fingers are tools without peer; but a steel or plastic hook is a useful accessory. A crochet hook will loop ends through areas too small for the fingers. Crocheting is a looping and chaining technique that is useful for creating free forms. Constructed of a single element, requiring no tension and no shed, crocheting will freely grow and develop through variations on chaining. Chain, single crochet, half-double,

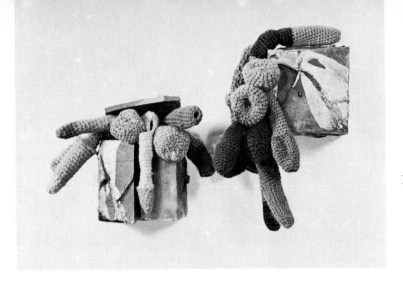

Fig. 49 *A Place for Everything
and Everything in its Place*
Shirley Marein. Ceramic raku
boxes, partially opened and
filled with crocheted forms in
browns, reds, oranges and
mixtures. Tight single crochet.
Photo Curt Meinel

double, treble and quadruple crochet are created from each
other. Single crochet is the firmest and tightest.

Start with a slip knot (fig. 50). With the crochet hook
through this loop and the wool wound around the index
finger of the opposite hand, catch a loop of yarn with the
hook and pull it through the slip knot. Each time this is
repeated the new loop remains on the hook and the previous
loop drops down as part of the chain. Make the chain the
desired length, then start back by putting the hook in the
second loop of the chain and pull out another loop on the
hook. There are now two loops on the crochet hook. Pull a
loop of yarn through the two loops for a completed single
crochet. Continue across row. At the end of the row add a
single chain and turn around to come back for the next row
(fig. 51).

Fig. 50 Slip knot

Perhaps the most interesting constructions can be arrived
at through tubular forms that increase and decrease in size
(fig. 49). Start with a chain of six or more loops. Make the
circle using a slip stitch. Insert the crochet hook under the
top threads of the second foundation chain stitch. Put the
yarn over the hook, draw through the foundation chain and
with one movement draw the yarn through both loops.
Work one row of slip stitch around the chain before starting
with single or double crochet.

To increase the circumference of the circular form, work
two stitches in the top threads of the same stitch of the
previous row. Increase gradually on each row for a smooth
circle.

Decrease by drawing up a single loop in the next top
thread of the previous row, then draw up another single
thread in the following top thread of the previous row;
place the yarn over the hook and draw through all three
loops on the hook.

Any stitch on the surface can be the start of a new surface.
When ending a thread, finish with a slip stitch.

Fig. 51 Single crochet

Macramé

Holding cord (knot bearer)   length of cord, dowel rod or other device around which knots are formed.

Reverse double half hitch or 'larks head'   pair of loops at the folded end of doubled over cords assembled for mounting.

Filler cords   vertical or horizontal cords forming a core for knotting.

Square knot   basic knot composed of four ends, two ends tied over and around the two filler ends, in two stages.

Half knot   half the square knot, tying one end over and through the other, starting from the same side each time.

Spiral sinnet (or sennit)   half knot tied repeatedly, causing a spiral.

Flat sinnet   square knots tied repeatedly that lie flat.

Half hitch   cord looped once around another cord or cords.

Double half hitch or clove hitch   cord looped twice around another cord or cords. The double half hitch may be worked horizontally, vertically or diagonally at angles of any degree.

Josephine knot or 'Carrick bend'   two fully formed loops interwoven with each other.

Picot   small loop extending beyond the work.

Macramé is a knotting technique as ancient as the need to tie strands together. Open to many interpretations, *macramé* is an Arabic word that probably evolved from the utilitarian purpose of tying off ends of warp threads after weaving, into a decorative fringe. The technique is still used decoratively but it is more important as a method of construction.

No extra equipment is needed for macramé. Most important, as with other construction forms, is the method of suspending or holding the cords. Large pieces can be suspended from a bar, smaller pieces worked on a macramé knotting board, such as the board used for warp twining (page 28), consisting of $\frac{1}{2}$ in. thick foam rubber, placed on a piece of masonite, covered with a towel held taut around the back with a whipping stitch. Cork board or any other composition board, soft enough to take a pin, will work equally well. The T-pin or a strong straight pin is essential. Metal rings, cork balls, beads, ceramic pieces and sticks of various kinds are additional adornments. Any kind of string, yarn, cord, twine, leather or synthetic cord can be used. Experiment with all of them. Wool with great elasticity is not entirely suitable for large hangings without supplementary support because of the tendency to sag. Smooth surfaced cords made of linen or cotton clearly show the design of the knotting. Very thick jute, cotton cordage or roving give quick results. Rayon satin rattail is sleek and shiny; braided rayon cord is lustrous and less shiny. Probably the most elegant of all fibres is braided nylon parachute cord with a filled core. The ends will fray disastrously if not seared. The best way to cut nylon is with an electrically heated wire or soldering knife that will cut and sear at the same time. A match flame leaves a burned edge hard to conceal. Marine supply shops or hardware stores are good sources of supply. All macramé knots are started with units of four ends or two lengths folded in half. Approximately eight times the desired finished length will be used up in knotting. The working ends of the square knot will be used up faster than the filler or core ends.

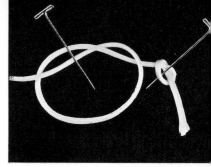

Fig. 52 Tie a holding cord on a board with overhand knots held in place with T-pins

Tie a holding cord on a board with overhand knots held in place with T-pins or strong straight pins (fig. 52). Tie two reverse double half hitches on the holding cord (figs 53 and 54). Hold the ends to a convenient working length by winding them around the fingers and securing with a rubber band. Allow about 18 in. of free working space. If the piece is large and a long cord length is necessary, keep the length sufficient but not unwieldy; add cords as needed. Do not carry cumbersome amounts of cord as this may become tangled or frayed and will hamper the knotting. Should a cord become hopelessly frayed, cut it off and add a new one.

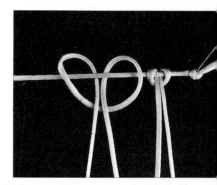

Fig. 53 Two reverse double half hitches in place on the holding cord

Stop knotting when the end is about 6 in. long. Splice a new cord to the 6 in. end. Place the new cord alongside the short end and work the two cords as one for a short distance; then drop the short end behind the work and continue with the new cord. The dropped end can be cut short at the conclusion of the work. A very slippery cord may need a drop of white glue to secure it on the reverse side.

The knot bearer cord must be kept steady and taut. In the working of horizontal bars it may be necessary to hold the knot bearer higher than the row above it to keep the rows flush. In the case of the diagonal knot bearing cord, it is a good idea to mark the position of the angle on the board.

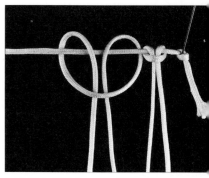

Fig. 54 Two reverse double half hitches backwards on the holding cord

Notes and score keeping are helpful when work is likely to be interrupted.

Macramé knots

Half knot

The half knot, the first part of the square knot, can be tied from left to right (fig. 55) or from right to left. The left-hand end cord is placed over the centre two filling cords; the right-hand end cord is placed over the left-hand cord, behind the filling cords and comes up and forward between the left-hand cord and the first filling cord. Grasp the two outside end cords and pull firmly to tighten the knot.

Fig. 55 Half knot

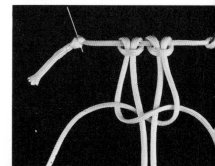

32

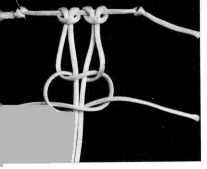

Fig. 56   Square knot

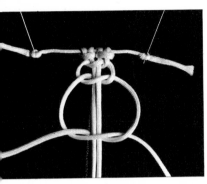

Fig. 57   Spiral sinnet

Square knot

The basic square knot is completed after the half knot is tied and tightened (fig. 56). Place the left-hand end cord behind the centre two filling cords, the right-hand end cord is placed under the left-hand cord, over the filling cords and down and out from between the left-hand cord and the first filling cord. Grasp the two outside end cords and tighten, pulling and pushing the knot upward.

The square knot is very versatile. It can be used as a gathering knot, grouping and holding any number of threads (fig. 59). In an alternating pattern, the square knot forms a tight or an open fabric (fig. 58), depending on the number of knots used. Alternate the pattern by square knotting across a row (two steps complete the square knot). On the second row, ignore the first two cords and start by knotting cords 3, 4, 5 and 6; continue across the row; the last two cords will be unused. On the third row of square knots again start with the outside end cord.

Spiral sinnet

The spiral sinnet is the half knot tied over and over again (fig. 57), always starting from the same side, placing the end cords over the filling cords. As the sinnet spirals (fig. 62), do not try to hold it flat, but turn with the spiral and knot on both sides of the sinnet.

Fig. 58   Square knot in an alternating pattern

Fig. 59   Square knot used to gather, group and hold

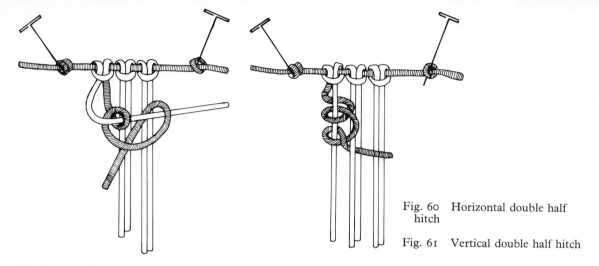

Fig. 60   Horizontal double half hitch

Fig. 61   Vertical double half hitch

Horizontal double half hitch

To make the horizontal double half hitch (fig. 60), starting from left to right: the end cord becomes a knot bearer placed over the top of the other cord or cords. The knot bearing cord must be held taut, a little higher than horizontal. The second cord coming from underneath is looped twice around the knot bearer in a half hitch.

Vertical double half hitch

In the vertical double half hitch (fig. 61) the knot bearing cord changes after each set of vertical double half hitches, but the cord constructing the double half hitches continues across the row. Starting from left to right, the end cord is the knotting cord, placed underneath the next vertical or knot bearing cord. The knotting cord comes from behind, loops around the vertical bearer cord and emerges down and in front of the loop. Repeat, remembering that all double half hitches are in sets of two. Hold the knot bearing cord taut in one hand and push the loops up and tighten. The first cord, continuing to be the knotting cord, is then placed under the third vertical; form two half hitches and tighten upwards. Continue across the row in this fashion, turning the corner with the same knotting cord, and knot the second row reversing the direction, placing the knotting cord under the vertical cord before starting the half hitches. The knotting cord will be used up rapidly; start a new cord by tying it to the short end on the reverse side.

Fig. 62   The flat sinnet of square knots and the spiral sinnet

Diagonal double half hitch

The diagonal double half hitch is the same as the horizontal double half hitch except that the angle of the knot bearing cord varies. In a symmetrical design the cords must be divided evenly, working from the outside into the centre or from the centre to the outside end. Figure 64 shows a hanging started with reverse double half hitches on a ring. The diagonal double half hitches at the top are worked from the centre to the outside end cord.

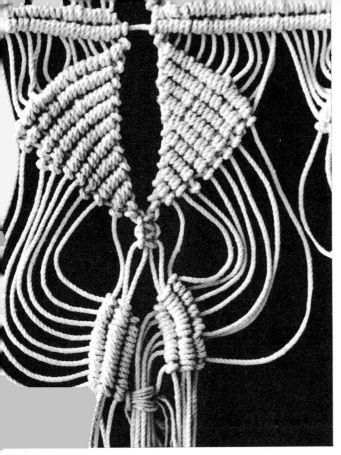

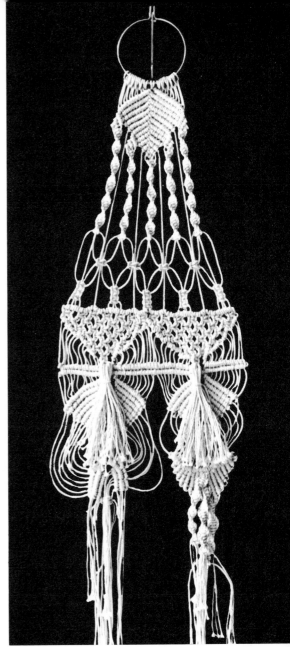

Above left
Fig. 63   Detail of figure 64, showing
  variations on the diagonal half hitch,
  worked from the centre to the outside,
  forming a slit

Above
Fig. 64   Hanging started with reverse
  double half hitches on a ring

Left
Fig. 65   *Trois Personnages* Aurelia Muñoz.
  Three-dimensional forms, approximately
  60 in. high, worked in horizontal and
  vertical double half hitches

Fig. 66 *Cartouche* Enid Russ.
White nylon and green ulstron
cord knotted on a wooden oval
frame of diagonal half hitches in
the round

Fig. 67 *Multicoloured Hanging*
Esther Gotthoffer. Linen and
cotton in natural, black, pink and
red, knotted in diagonal double
half hitches. The colours are
arranged symmetrically: four
reverse double half hitches of
black, four of natural, two of
pink, four red, two pink, four
natural, ending with four reverse
double half hitches of black—a
total of 48 ends. The colours
move from side to side by
sometimes acting as knot bearers
and other times as knotting cords.
The double half hitches must be
pulled up firmly and tightened
very close to each other in order
to cover a knot-bearing cord of a
contrasting colour

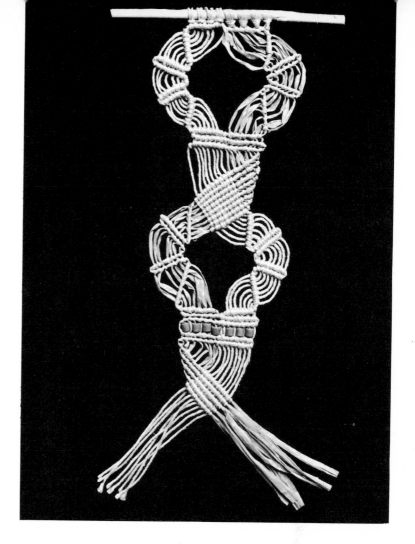

Fig. 68 Hanging by Esther
Gotthoffer. Natural coloured
linen with pink raffia and small
beads. The raffia is transposed
from one side to the other with
diagonal double half hitches

Determine and mark the angle you desire on the board.
Place your hand holding the taut knot bearer cord at the
marked point for each successive row.

For a solid fabric without openings, knot all the vertical
cords in the left half over the first cord from the right-hand
half, beginning at the centre. Drop the knotting cord when
you reach the outside left end and pick up the first vertical
from centre left, holding it taut at the marked point on the
right side; double half hitch across to the right. Drop the
knotting cord at the right outside end. Use up all the
verticals alternating from side to side—in this way all of the
right-hand cords will be transposed to the left side and the
left-hand cords to the right side. This is the method used
for moving colours.

The transposed ends are then knotted in a series of spiral-
ling sinnets alternating with a single free cord. The ends are
then gathered together with square knots in a series of

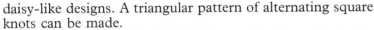

Fig. 69 Josephine knot or Carrick bend

daisy-like designs. A triangular pattern of alternating square knots can be made.

The diagonal double half hitch can also be made in the form of an x (fig. 70): notice the soft textural quality that wool imparts to knotting. The x form is worked in groups of eight cords in an alternating pattern. Cord 1 on the left and cord 8 on the right approach the centre simultaneously. At the intersection the knot bearers are joined; cord 1 is knotted in double half hitches over cord 8 and continues as a knot bearer to the right and cord 8 proceeds to the left.

Josephine knot or Carrick bend

The Josephine knot (fig. 69) may be tied with any number of cords. A good way to practise is with two contrasting colours. Make a large loop with one colour, pass the other colour over the loop, under the end, over the next section of the loop, under the next, over the contrasting colour and under the last section; then gently tighten the parts. Remember that the procedure is over, under, over, under, over, under.

Picot

Decorative edges can be worked from the top, bottom or sides towards the centre using picots and eliminating fringes. A picot is made by folding two lengths in half, pinning the loops to a knotting board and joining the ends with square knots (fig. 72). Beginning with a single set of picots or multiple picots is often desirable in making necklaces.

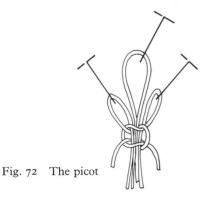

Fig. 70 Diagonal double half hitch in the form of an X

Fig. 71 Section of a belt with Josephine knots alternating with a chain of half hitches: the Josephine knots are made with six cords; the chain of half hitches consists of two cords, one looped alternately over the other

Fig. 72 The picot

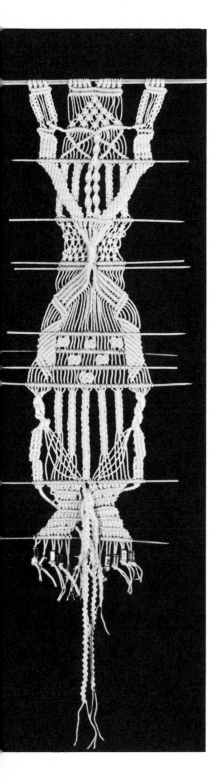

Fig. 73 Wall-hanging by Janet Silberstein. Nylon braided cord with Japanese hibachi sticks, weighted at the bottom with small hollow copper beads

Fig. 74 From the sketchbook of Janet Silberstein

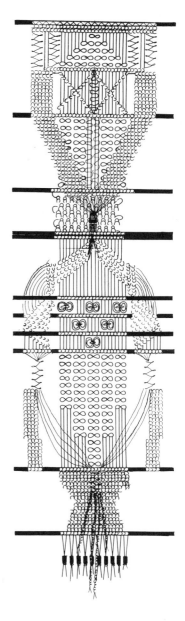

LEGEND

∨∨ Lark's Head Mounting

ⵛⵛⵛ Horizontal Clove Hitch

ⴹⴹⴹ Vertical Clove Hitch

∞ Square Knot

≍ Alternative Clove Hitch Chain

🙾 Josephine Knot

▤ Wrapping

The pattern draft

Some people approach their materials with emotional intensity and work with them directly, gathering inspiration from texture, colour and developing forms; others keep sketch books, gathering inspiration from nature or while daydreaming. Many people working on a large scale for exhibitions or to a commissioned design have assistants and work from a model or maquette.

Fig. 75 *Peace Dance* David
Holbourne. Base of bound coiled
rope covered with half hitches
and Ghiordes knots in
polypropylene rope and sisal

Fig. 76 *Winged Forms* Robert
Mabon. Woven dimensional
form, with additional macramé
ribs in sisal

Pattern drafts, indicating the colour and placement of threads, vary according to the symbols used. Develop symbols that you can identify easily. Macramé is versatile, adapting to many construction forms, and it can be used in combination with other media.

3 Planning a design

Fig. 77 Visual communication symbol derived from the circular form of the eye

When planning a design remember that yarns and fibres are structurally forceful materials. Emotional content and form are innate in the fibres themselves and they are often at their best with little superimposed design. Most weavers do have an inner sympathy for the unique character of the materials and they stress sculptural construction.

In addition to the structure of fibre, colours—both natural and chemically produced—are stimulating. Plan on dyeing and redyeing; plying the wools and plying again.

Great weaving traditions arise in areas topographically suited to the natural resources necessary to the development of the craft. The high plateaus of the Andean range of Peru support the alpaca, llama, vicuna and sheep; cotton is easily grown in the coastal areas. The Oriental rug tradition, continuous from antiquity to the present day, is based on the climate of the high plateaus of Central Asia and the magnificence of the Persian lamb together with agreeable conditions for the development of silkworms. Wool, jute, hemp, sisal, cotton, horsehair, alpaca, cashmere, silk, fibre-glass, raffia, sticks and stones, and all metal and chemical fibres are available to everyone.

Fig. 78 Sea urchin: a natural source of design with rhythmic circular form and textural interest

Fig. 79 Tapestry-woven form developed from the circle

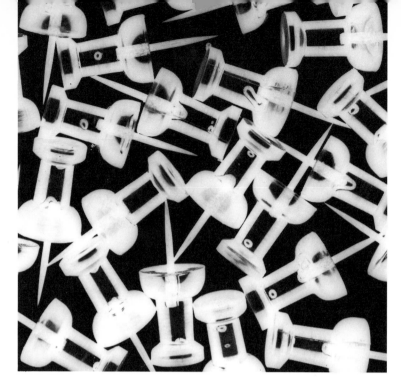

Fig. 80 Common everyday objects, such as pushpins (recorded here by scattering on sensitized paper and exposing to light) suggest forms that might otherwise go unnoticed

Fig. 81 Wall-hanging by Melissa Cornfeld. Geometric rectangular design worked from a preliminary cut-paper sketch

Though the materials present the basic inspiration and determine much of the visual presence in a fibre construction, still the overall form must be taken into account. Without an elaborate art-school background, the bird builds a nest that functions, is geometrically perfect, and has a positive form in space. The wasp's nest and the beehive are hollow cylinders, and of course there is no shape more beautiful than the ovoid of the egg. The basic geometric forms are starting points for endless variations whether you are influenced by nature or by the symbols of contemporary media. A simple design of subtle proportions with the textural interests of the materials is exciting. Study the circle, the iris of the eye, concentric circles rippling the surface of water, a cabbage, the radiating sun, a blowfish. Observe and analyse form and the design potential in everything around you from the mechanical cleverness of the paperclip to the complexity of the human form.

A sketch may be flat, often colourless and with little depth. Cut paper is possibly a better medium. Colour-aid and construction papers are available in a wide range of colours. Paper of course is flexible, easy to cut, change, discard and move about. But drawing or constructing a design with the collage method has limitations because the character of the materials and the final method of structuring is so different. Whatever approach you choose, recognize it as a point of departure. There is no formula for creativity. Freedom from restraints, intuition and an understanding of your craft will contribute to highly individual works of art.

4   The dyeing process

Dyestuff   material yielding dye.
Dyebath   liquid yielded by dye material and water.
Mordant   substance which creates an affinity between dye and fibre.
Exhaust   cause total absorption of colour from dyebath.
Overdyeing   dyeing over previously dyed area with the same or another colour.
Wetting out   thoroughly soaking fibres before dyeing.

Unquestionably, commercial dyes are foolproof, cheaper, faster and the colours more brilliant, but vegetable dyeing is more fun. The emotional involvement in vegetable dyeing generates excitement and gives a sense of exploration and discovery. Experiments are possible for the town dweller and suburbanite as well as for those who live in the country. Craftsmen in large cities do not have abundant vegetation with which to work but many common household items yield a great variety of colours; the shells of nuts, the skins of onions, red cabbage, or the petals from a floral bouquet. Pine cones are for sale in the market at Christmas time in most cities: dust them off, break into little pieces, soak for a few days in softened water and boil. The aromatic odour is pleasantly nostalgic. Some fir trees yield a good dye. Why not try the tips of your Christmas spruce? Does the bark have any potential? Try everything. The Greeks on the island of Crete dry and save the skins of lemons and oranges. A substantial accumulation will yield a beautiful yellow and orange colour.

The most exotic dyes are easiest to obtain from chemical houses in the cities. Cochineal, for instance, extracted from a scale insect found on certain cactus plants in dry country, is a natural dye source for a wide range of reds and purples. Indigo, too, the traditional source of blue, is easily purchased.

Natural dyes may be animal, vegetable or mineral. Most natural materials require interaction with minerals to release the colour, and to make the yarn receptive to the dye. This addition is called a mordant, the process by which the colour is set or fixed in the fibre.

Do not be intimidated by complicated texts on vegetable dyeing. Rule of thumb is an equal weight of plant material to an equal weight of yarn (for two ounces of wool you will need two ounces of onion skins).

Invest in a book on the wild flowers that grow in your general geographic area. Select a book with colour plates from which you can identify the flowers by their common names. Wild flowers are disappearing from the suburbs, and many older texts on natural dyestuffs list plants, such as Bloodroot, the Indian source for orange-red, which is now cultivated and sold through rare-plant dealers. Remember that a plant is only a weed when it grows where it is not wanted.

There are many surprises in store from the vegetation around you. Some leaves and flowers give up more or less dye and the quantity can be adjusted accordingly. Try everything—there is no way to tell what the yield will be. The Japanese red maple produces a delicate blue violet, whereas the brilliant dark red copper beech, after hours of boiling, produces a medium sienna more easily arrived at with pecan hulls.

Draw no conclusions from exterior appearances; try everything including roots and bark; try different mordants. Results are always different even with the same plant because of differences in the time of year, in the soil, in the atmosphere.

General rules for dyeing

Here are some general rules for dyeing that are quite flexible. Your aim may or may not be to dye evenly, but it is a good idea to start with clean wool because a greasy surface impairs the receptivity.

1 If using unspun wool fleece, carefully tease it. Pull it apart so that it is not matted before dyeing. (The expression 'dyed in the wool' describes the saturation of the wool with dye before combing or carding and spinning.)

2 Wind your wool continuously into skeins on a swift if you have one, or around the back of a chair. Keep the ball of wool in a bowl on the floor to prevent it rolling about.

3 It is a good idea to experiment with small quantities of yarn. About six yards of a white 2-ply rug wool is adequate for a colour sample. Remember that natural or slightly coloured wool will dye to slightly different tonal values.

4 Cut three eight-inch pieces of cotton string; tie them loosely around the skein in several places to keep the wool from tangling during the dyeing process. Tying with cotton string is a good idea in order to see the effect of the dye on cotton.

5 Wash the wool in cold water with mild soap suds by swishing gently around in an enamel basin; rinse, change water and allow to soak in clear water in preparation for dyeing and applying mordant. Wet wool is most receptive

to mordant and to dye.

6   Make sure the wool is fully submerged whenever it is in a bath.

7   Always rinse between steps.

8   Some references say dry in the shade, others in the sun. It doesn't seem to make much difference and if the colour has a tendency to fade in bright light it is probably better to find out immediately. In winter, drying near the boiler or over a radiator works well.

9   Never actively boil the wool because it hardens it; keep the water at a point at which it is just beginning to simmer.

10   Do not stir vigorously, move the wool about gently.

11   Use an enamel, copper or iron basin, plastic measuring spoons and cups; use a glass rod, dowel or chopstick to stir and lift the wool. Always keep utensils for dyeing separate from cooking equipment as some of the chemicals are poisonous.

Mordants

Preparation with mordant may be done just before dyeing, or it can be done in advance and the wool kept dry until needed. The mordant can also be dissolved in the dye infusion at the conclusion of the plant boiling.

For most light colours alum is a successful mordant (potassium aluminium sulphate), for dark colours use iron (ferrous sulphate of copperas). There are two other useful mordants: tin (stannous chloride or crystals of tin) and chrome (bichromate of potash). Keep the wool that has been treated with alum, tin or chrome mordant, dry, labelled and in readiness. Iron is usually put directly into the dye bath. Household cream of tartar is a brightener and is used with many of the mordants. There are some plants that need no mordant because of their naturally high tannic acid content. Dandelions are high in tannic acid and the dye is set in the yarn with no additional mordant. It is helpful to use vinegar, salt or acetic acid as an aid to colour fastness. Wool dyed with pokeberries fades in time and a generous amount of added vinegar is helpful. Do not confuse the use of a mordant, designed to keep colour from bleeding out of the fibre, with the problem of colour fastness or fading due to bright light and sun.

The following amounts of mordant are suitable for 1 lb of wool in 4 gallons of water:

Alum

3 oz. potassium aluminium (different and more functional than ammonium aluminium, a household astringent) and 1 oz. cream of tartar dissolved in warm water. Dissolve in a plastic container before stirring into the 4 gallon mordanting basin.

Tin
$\frac{1}{2}$ oz. tin crystals (stannous chloride) to $\frac{1}{2}$ oz. cream of tartar dissolved in hot water in a plastic container. Tin is essential to reds and oranges. The amounts can vary from recipe to recipe as can the additional substances needed.

Chrome
$\frac{1}{2}$ oz. chrome (potassium bichromate or dichromate, also called bichromate of potash) dissolved in half a cup of hot water in a plastic container. For even dyeing it is advisable to use the wool prepared with chrome immediately. Keep the lid on the pot while simmering with chrome.

Do not be put off by these measures. Remember that ounces may be measured in tablespoons depending upon the weight of the material. For a test sample of about 6 yards, the amount of tin necessary would only be a few crystals on the tip of a plastic spoon. Too much tin can make the wool harsh and stiff; chrome is very sensitive to light and can impair the colour; and too much iron has a tendency to darken and harden the wool. Too much alum results in stickiness. Alum has the effect of adding a slight amount of yellow to dye, sometimes desirable. Use the mordants sparingly.

Collecting and extracting colour from the dye material
Collect your dyestuff over a period of time. The dry outer skins of onions are quite odourless and can be saved in a plastic bag. Nut shells can also be accumulated over a period of time. Some plants and roots are easy to dry and save until needed but most plants are at their best fresh. In the fresh state a smaller amount is needed. Store fresh plants and leafy material in plastic bags in a cold place until you are ready to use them. They will maintain their freshness for at least a month if kept in a refrigerator. Do not hesitate to freeze berries and other materials, either fresh or after partial boiling. Label everything with identification of contents and the date packaged. Most plants are not edible.

Prepare the material by breaking it up into small pieces and soaking it in soft water. Rain water is best because it contains no additional chemicals. Commercial water softeners are also good. Fresh flowers and leaves require little soaking, a few hours or overnight is enough. Petals can be used immediately without soaking. Anything that is dried, hard or woody must be soaked, sometimes as long as a week. Make certain that the material is covered by the water, stir or turn over the material in the water occasionally. Soak materials in the same pot you intend to use for the boiling.

A little experience is necessary to determine the type of container to select. An enamel basin can, of course, be used for almost everything and is particularly suitable for light clear colours. Aluminium and galvanized utensils are not suitable. A copper pot is helpful in producing rich burnished colours like sienna and mustard. Cochineal develops more intensity in a copper pot. An iron kettle is reserved for browns and blacks as the additional iron darkens the colour. Iron is in itself a colouring oxide.

Dyeing the wool

The water containing the dye materials should be heated to boiling point and maintained just under boiling point to curtail evaporation. A pinch of alum will start the flow of colour from soft vegetation. Simmer for about thirty minutes for leaves and flowers, longer for bark and hulls. The plant material should be strained out at the end of the simmering period, although it is quite possible to enter the washed, prepared with mordant and wetted wool with the plant material and wash the plant material out with the first rinsing. It may take an hour for a colour of sufficient depth to develop.

Do not stir vigorously; move the wool around in the bath with a stick. To test for colour lift the wool from the water on a stick and pinch between thumb and index finger to remove the moisture. Wet wool always looks darker than dry wool and by squeezing out some of the water you will see an approximation of the dry colour. The wool may be left to cool in the water or removed and rinsed immediately. Try to keep the water temperatures for each process about the same. Do not plunge the wool into icy water when it has just emerged from boiling water. Rinse several times until the water is clear.

It is a good idea to rinse in soapy water, particularly when the mordants have been added to the dye bath. The chances of irritation are lessened and the wool will be softer to the touch. Hang the skeins to dry. Fleece should be spread out on brown wrapping paper or a vinyl cloth and turned several times. When you have finished dyeing wash the dye pots thoroughly. If the dye has not been thoroughly exhausted it may be saved in labelled jars to be used again. Vegetable dyes should be stored in the refrigerator or some other cool place because of the tendency to develop mould—although the mould does not impair the quality of the dye and can be skimmed off before using again.

Yarn samples

When the skeins are thoroughly dry remove the cotton holding cords. Hold the skein taut between your two outstretched index fingers. Turning one index finger clockwise and the other finger counter clockwise, twist the yarn tight. Bring the two fingers together. The yarn folded in half will cause the bottom to ply around itself. Insert the loop from one finger into the loop on the other finger. Remove. To make labels, cut a 3 × 5 in. index card into thirds. Print the name of the plant material, the mordant used, the type of kettle and any other pertinent information. Thread a needle with a cotton cord, pierce through the labelling card and through the single loop at the top of the yarn. Remove needle and tie ends in an overhand knot. Allow the sample of yarn to remain exposed in a normally lit room for two weeks, note any changes on the back of the card. A well labelled yarn sample is invaluable.

Recipes for dyes

Pine cones (*Pinus*)
medium tan, colour of pine cones
1 lb. wool
1½ lb. pine cones
Break the cones into small pieces; soak for several days. Boil the liquid for two hours in an iron kettle; enter the wetted wool treated with alum mordant. The addition of iron (ferrous sulphate) will produce a dark brown.

Fig. 82   Pine cones

Onion skins (*Allium cepa*)
burnt orange
1 lb. wool
1 lb. dry outer onion skins
Soak onion skins in softened water in a copper pot overnight. Strain and return liquid to copper pot. Enter wetted wool treated with alum mordant; simmer for thirty minutes. Remove, rinse and dry. To make the colour lightfast enter the wool, dried and wetted out again, in the dyebath, bring to a simmer. Repeat several times. Rinse and dry between each dipping. A variety of tints and tones can be obtained from onion skin dye by using different mordants. Try chrome.

Fig. 83   Onion skins

Bracken (*Pteridium aquilinum*)
light yellow to yellow-green
1 lb. wool
1 lb. fresh fronds
Bracken, a single frond fern, is at its best in the early spring when the shoots are still coiled at the top. Simmer for two hours in an enamel basin. Strain and replenish evaporated water. Enter the wool treated with alum. Simmer for one hour.

Fig. 84   Bracken

48

Fig. 85   Pecan hulls

Fig. 86   Walnut shells

Fig. 87   Japanese Red Maple leaves

Fig. 88   Rhododendron leaves

Pecan hulls (*Carya illinoensis, Hicoria pecan*)
medium burnt sienna, warm toast colour
1 lb. wool
2 lb. dry hulls
Alum and cream of tartar mordant
Cover broken hulls with soft water in an iron kettle. Soak for several days. Simmer for an hour, adding water as needed to keep the hulls covered. Strain, return the liquid to the same kettle, add water, enter wetted wool, simmer for about an hour. Rinse well and hang skeins to dry.

Walnut shells (*Juglans regia*)
various shades of brown
1 lb. wool
2 lb. dry shells
Proceed as for pecan hulls. A mordant is not necessary with walnut shells, but if the colour is not dark enough add one tablespoon of alum to the dye water. Variety of colour depends on the quantity of shells used. For a more even colour, keep the wool immersed in the water while it is simmering.

Japanese Red Maple leaves (*Acer palmatum*)
lavender
1 lb. wool
1 lb. leaves and branch tips
Tear up leaves and break up soft branch tips. Soak overnight in soft water. Use an enamel basin. Boil for half an hour with a pinch of alum to make the colour flow. Strain. Return the dye liquid to the basin, add a quarter teaspoon of iron (ferrous sulphate). Enter wetted wool and simmer. Test for colour after half an hour. More iron will turn the colour a dark warm grey-brown. If the colour is not dark enough, leave the wool to cool in the dyebath.

Rhododendron leaves (*Rhododendron maximum*)
shades of grey
1 lb. wool
2 lb. leaves
1 oz. iron
Cut up leaves of the rhododendron bush and soak for a few days in an iron kettle. Boil for about two hours; strain and return dye liquid to iron kettle. Add water if the liquid has evaporated in the boiling. Add 1 oz. of iron sulphate, allow it to dissolve and add the wetted wool. Simmer for half an hour. Test colour. Return to the dye bath for deeper colour or remove, rinse thoroughly and hang skeins to dry. Successive skeins can be dyed in the same bath, becoming progressively lighter in tone each dipping. Add water to counteract evaporation and simmer for half an hour each time.

Milkweed (*Asclepiadaceae, Asclepias syriaca L*)
soft medium green to yellow green
1 lb. wool
1 lb. leaves or leaves and flowers
Break up leaves and flowers, soak for several days in soft water in an enamel or copper basin, preferably a copper basin. Bring material to the boil, then simmer for an hour. Strain. Try alum mordanted wool with a small amount of ferrous sulphate of copperas for a soft clear green. Wool mordanted with chrome will turn from a brass yellow in the milkweed dyebath with the addition of ferrous sulphate. Household ammonia is another addition, turning the alum mordanted wool to tan and the chrome mordanted wool to a stronger yellow orange.

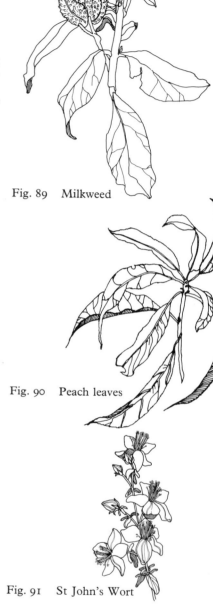

Fig. 89   Milkweed

Peach leaves (*Persica*)
burnt golden orange
1 lb. wool
1 lb. peach leaves
Break up leaves and allow to soak in a copper pot for about two weeks. Fermentation will take place but the mould is not detrimental. Simmer for half an hour adding water as needed. Add warm and wetted wool, that has been pre-mordanted with chrome, to an equally warm dyebath. Raise the temperature of the water slowly and maintain at a simmer under boiling point until the desired colour is reached. An afterbath of ferrous sulphate will turn the colour to a rich brown.

Fig. 90   Peach leaves

St John's Wort (*Guttiferae, Hypericum perforatum L.*)
from yellow to deep mustard through greens to red
1 lb. wool
1 lb. fresh plant material
Use the top leafy quarter of the total plant including the tiny yellow flower heads. Cut up and soak overnight in rain water or softened water. Boil in a copper pot for about half an hour, add tin crystals (stannous chloride) and cream of tartar for mustard yellow; a few grains of iron for a darker colour. Red can be produced with tin crystals and oxalic acid; try an ammonia afterbath for olive green. In an enamel basin, mordanted with alum, St John's Wort will produce a strong yellow. Test all mordants and pots.

Fig. 91   St John's Wort

Buttercups (*Ranunculaceae, Ranunculus acris L.*)
yellow
1 lb. wool
1 lb. fresh plant material
Extract the colour in the same way as for bracken. Buttercup extract makes an excellent overdye for yarn dyed with the extract from the bracken fronds. The overdyeing produces a strong bright yellow that is lightfast.

Fig. 92   Buttercups

Cochineal (*Dactylopius coccus*)
red to purple
1 lb. wool
2½ oz. powdered cochineal
½ oz. chrome
1 teaspoon vinegar
For purple, mordant the wool in advance with chrome. Simmer wool in chrome bath for one hour, keeping wool submerged (put a plate on top of it); rinse and keep in water until dye is ready. Using the copper pot, bring the cochineal and vinegar to the boil, stir until the ingredients are dissolved. Add the treated wool and simmer for an hour. Allow the wool to remain in the dyebath until cooled. Rinse until water is clear. Hang skeins to dry. For red, mordant with alum and cream of tartar. For a slightly different red, add quarter of a teaspoon of tin crystals to the alum and cream of tartar. An iron mordant will result in a strong violet.

There are many more plants and trees to explore: privet clippings (*Ligustrum vulgare*); golden-rod flowers (*Solidago*); marigold flowers (*Tagetes*); pear tree leaves (*Pyrus communis*); lily of the valley leaves (*Convallaria majalis*); bay leaves (*Myrica pensylvanica*); ginkgo tree bark (*Ginkgo biloba*); azalea leaves (*Rhododendron japonicum*); oak leaves and acorns (*Quercus velutina*); grapes and vine leaves (*Vitis*); myrtle leaves (*Myrtus*); juniper (*Juniperus*); sumac (*Rhus glabra*); tea and coffee; and other plants indigenous to your area.

Matching dye lots at different times with different batches of plant material is always exceedingly difficult. Soils differ, the time of year when the plant is picked affects its dye potential, as does the quality of the water, the pot and the atmosphere. But the soft colours of vegetable origin are in keeping with each other. Either dye enough for a project or accept the differences in dye lots and take advantage of the harmonic vagaries of vegetable dyeing.

Commercial dyes

Commercial dyes are designed to work with a variety of fibres. The same dye will be suitable for wool, linen, cotton and silk as well as synthetic fibres. Commercial dyes are easy to use and require little or no boiling. Follow the directions on the package.

Here are some points to consider before you start the dyeing process.

1 Soak the wool in water before dyeing. Use enough water so that the yarn is not cramped for space. It needs enough water to swim freely.

2 Before you enter the entire hank of yarn test for colour with a strand of yarn pulled loose from the main strand. Squeeze the piece of yarn between your thumb and index finger. With the water pressed out, the wool will appear almost the way it does when dry.

3 The yarn can be dyed in scalding hot tap water at least 150°F (63°C), but most colours, particularly dark colours are best simmered for thirty minutes. If using scalding tap water let the yarn soak for at least an hour or until the water cools. The continued heat helps the lightfast quality. Steaming does not hurt the yarn.

4 Use small quantities of dye for light colours.

5 With dip-dyeing a skein of yarn can have variation in colour. For instance, pull strands from the centre and dip a skein of orange into red dye. Dip ends into a khaki colour (created by adding green, the complement of orange, to the orange dyebath) for a mottling effect.

6 Double dip-dyeing gives greater depth. Dye light and re-dye; this can be done several times.

7 Colours can be blended and mellowed. Start with a pale tinted base colour or, at the conclusion of the dyeing, re-dye all the colours in a neutral colour dyebath, which gives an antique effect. For a neutralizing effect make a weak greying or mellowing solution in advance and keep it on hand. A small amount of blue, brown and orange in a quart of water is suitable.

8 All bits and pieces and mistakes can be dyed black. Try not to make too many mistakes or you will have on hand an overwhelming amount of black yarn.

5   Constructing a fabric

Fig. 93   Combs for beating the weft (*from top to bottom*): English dog currying comb; Mexican wooden comb; Afro comb from Tanganyika; small steel comb; Nilus Leclerc tapestry comb; Mexican wooden comb

Loom   frame for holding warp threads taut.

Shed   space formed to hold weft when alternate warp threads are raised.

Shed sticks   wide flat sticks for separating the sheds and holding them open.

Heddles   string loops through which the warp is threaded to aid in changing the shed.

Heddle bar   dowel or stick for holding and lifting the heddles.

Sword stick   bevel-edged stick, same size as a shed stick, to hold open the shed raised by the heddles or to batten or pack down the weft.

Shuttle   tool for containing and carrying the weft thread.

Pick-up stick   smooth stick, sometimes pointed or hooked at one end, for picking up warp threads for special pattern designs; also used for looping.

Pick or **shot**   single row of weft; pick and weft used interchangeably.

Selvedge (selvage)   woven edges often strengthened with double warp threads.

Bubbling   putting the weft across the row in a series of small arcs so that the weft will not be too tight causing the warp to pull into an hourglass form.

Beat   to pack the weft tightly into the shed.

Tabby   from the Arabic word *attabi*, the weavers' quarters in Baghdad, meaning a plain weave; the warp and the weft are equally visible, a balanced 50/50 weave.

Anything that can be woven on a complex contemporary loom can also be woven on a primitive loom. Weaving without a loom is an expression used loosely: any device that will hold the warp threads under tension is a loom. Finger weaving must be attached at one end and held taut in the hands. A fisherman makes netting by looping the cord around his big toe. The Greeks threw the warp over a bar and attached weights to groups of threads at the bottom. A backstrap loom consists of five sticks; after warping, the upper stick is tied to a tree and the lower bar tied around the back of the weaver with a strap and held taut by the weaver's distance from the tree. Every known technique was used to construct Peruvian textiles. Modern technology has

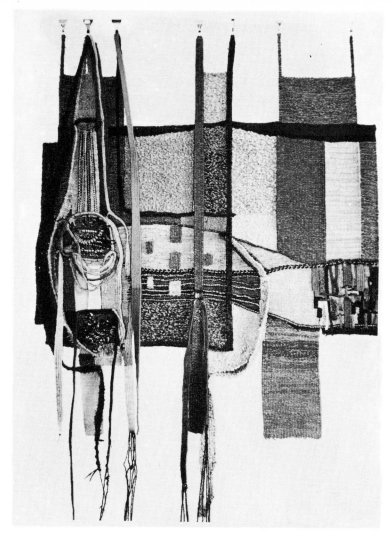

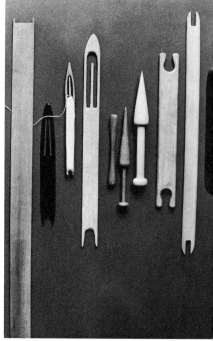

increased the speed of production but the basic methods
remain the same.

The word 'weaving' defines many purposes: the contemporary meaning must include the element of intense
personal involvement. The activity is both the process and
pleasure of weaving.

The inkle loom

Inkle weaving is warp faced weaving with a hidden weft. It
is basically a plain weave with designs obtained by picking
up threads from the lower warp. Very little is known about
the origin of the word 'inkle'. It sounds so much like the
middle-English word 'inkling', meaning to communicate a
vague notion, that there is inconclusive speculation that it

may be Welsh or Scottish in origin. The inkle loom weaves a narrow band and has been in use for a long time. A circular warp wound around pegs is basic, primitive and universal, serving functional and decorative needs. Contemporary English and American inkle looms are portable, comfortable and easy to use for learning very clearly and simply the principles of weaving.

Build your own inkle loom (fig. 96). If you have never handled tools, the experience and confidence gained is inestimable. You will need:

Pine shelving, 6 in. wide, 30 to 36 in. long (not longer than your arm can reach)
Dowel, $\frac{5}{8}$ in. thick, 36 in. long (to be cut in five equal pieces)
Wood, $1 \times 3 \times 30$ in. (to be cut in three equal pieces as upright supports for the dowels)
Nine $1\frac{1}{2}$ in. screws

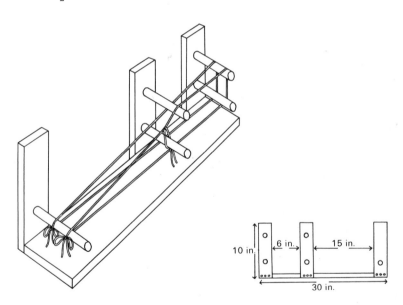

Fig. 96 Plan for an inkle loom

To assemble, attach the three upright supports to the pine shelving with nine $1\frac{1}{2}$ in. screws, three in each section for sturdiness. A stretched warp has tremendous pull and the problem is to keep the supports upright and the dowels in alignment. Drill the holes to fit the dowels accurately. Dip each dowel in white glue before inserting for a tight and secure fit.

This is a basic and inexpensive plan for an inkle loom. You will be able to think of many refinements and improvements. For instance, longer dowels of a heavier weight will support a wider piece of weaving. Another single dowel inserted in a support placed directly behind the second set of dowels, midway between the two, will add extra length to the yardage of the warp.

The heddle

The shed can be changed by picking up every other thread with the fingers as described in finger weaving; but a small loop of string, called a heddle, through which every other warp thread is passed, opens the shed in unison. When the heddles are attached to a heddle bar the shed is held open, freeing the hands for working the weft thread. There are many ways to measure and tie the heddles. Remember that you will need half as many heddles as there are warp threads because a shed is opened by lifting or depressing alternate threads. Heddles for the inkle loom are individual loops measuring half the distance between the two dowels on the middle support. They will be attached to the bottom dowel of the middle support.

Determine the distance between the dowels, allow some extra length because of the take up when the loop is placed around the bottom dowel and mark the measurement on a piece of scrap wood. Hammer two long finishing nails (nails without heads) into the wood at these points, half way down so that the nails stand free. These finishing nails, used as measures, may be placed directly on the bottom shelving of the loom, to be removed when the heddles have been completed. Use polished linen or strong smooth cotton string; loop the string around the two nails and tie the ends in a square knot (fig. 97); cut about two inches from the knot, remove and tie another. The heddles may also be made by tying and knotting them around a cardboard gauge. Plan to use the heddles over and over again. Thread the heddles on a string or on to a large safety-pin when not in use, so they will not be lost.

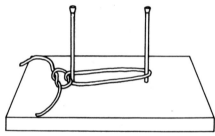

Fig. 97   Tying a heddle

Choosing fibres

In general, fibres are either natural or synthetic. Natural fibres are derived directly from the source: wool from sheep, silk from the silkworm. Cotton, flax (linen), jute and hemp are vegetable fibres. Rayon is a man-made fibre developed from wood and cotton. Nylon, polyesters and vinyls are artificial yarns developed through scientific research with mineral and chemical ingredients.

In choosing a warp for the inkle loom almost any type of yarn that is strong and smooth may be used. Fuzzy, hairy yarns should be avoided in an inkle warp. The affinity of fuzzy threads for each other makes opening the shed difficult. Very nubby threads can also be trying. Novelty threads of this type are best used as weft. Although intricate detail does require finer threads, a strong 2- or 3-ply wool is faster and simpler for the very first effort.

The pattern draft

Inkle weaving is warp faced, the weft completely hidden except at the very edge of the selvedge; the colour and arrangement of the warp, therefore, determine the pattern design. If all the heddles were threaded with white yarn and all the open spaces between heddles with black yarn, the woven pattern would be of black and white horizontal bars. Horizontal bars, vertical bars and alternating squares (the checkerboard pattern) are the basic designs from which all combinations and variations are made (fig. 98). As an aid in setting up the loom draw a pattern draft of the colours and their placement on graph paper (fig. 99). The top row of squares indicates the threading of the heddles, the bottom row, threading through the open spaces between heddles. Colour possibilities are unlimited and are identified by symbols.

Warping the inkle loom

Start the threading in the open space. When the warp is of heavy yarn, it is not necessary to strengthen the edge with a selvedge. If a selvedge is necessary, thread two warp threads alongside each other in the open space, then proceed according to the pattern draft. Repeat the double selvedge threading at the far end. An inkle warp is circular. The warp thread proceeds from the single front dowel over and around the back dowels and returns underneath to the single front dowel. The circular warp travels around the dowels as it is woven; it must, therefore, be free. Begin by passing the first thread over the front dowel, through the space between the dowels of the second set of supports; then over the top of the back dowel and around the outside of the lower dowel of the back set. Carry the thread back to the front again. Draw the top and bottom of the yarn towards you about 10 in. beyond

Fig. 98   Staggered horizontal bars

Fig. 99   Drafting a pattern: *top*, horizontal bars; *middle*, vertical bars; *bottom*, alternating squares. The pattern is read from left to right, then repeated in reverse from the centre line to the selvedge. Each symbol represents a different colour

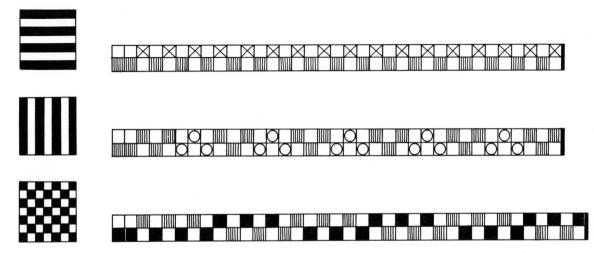

the front dowel; cut, tie, adjust the tension and finish the tying in a bow. Draw the second thread through a heddle, place the heddle on the lower bar of the middle set of supports. Run this thread up over the top bar, over and around the back set of dowels, along the bottom to the front dowel. Cut, tie, adjust the tension and tie a bow against the front bar. Repeat these two steps until the desired width is reached. The extra length of the bows against the front bar is helpful in releasing the tension as the weft takes up the warp and is also helpful in finishing the piece. Tighten and re-tie the bows should any of the warp threads loosen during the weaving.

Weaving
Cut two pieces of cardboard about $\frac{1}{2} \times 5$ in. Place one piece in the open shed; change the shed by placing the flat of the hand, palm down, behind the second set of dowels and depressing the warp. Open the shed in front of the heddle bar with the other hand, palm up (fig. 100). Run your hand, holding the set of warp threads, through the shed towards the cardboard. Insert the second piece of cardboard. The pieces of cardboard tend to stabilize and space the threads.

It is a good idea to select a weft thread, of any weight, that will match the colour of the warp at the edges. Wind the weft around a shuttle. An inexpensive shuttle can be made of cardboard. Cut a length of cardboard about 2 in. wide and longer than the width of the warp threads. Notch the ends to keep the wool from slipping off. The long side of a good shuttle for inkle weaving is tapered and smoothly sanded, and can also be used as a beater. Do not overload the shuttle with thread—it must pass easily through the open shed. Change the shed behind the second cardboard by placing the hand, palm up, behind the second set of dowels and pull up the depressed warp threads. Insert the index

Fig. 100   The open shed: the dark
   threads are depressed, bringing
   the white threads to the top

Fig. 101   Adjusting the weft
   thread by riding it back and
   forth across the shed

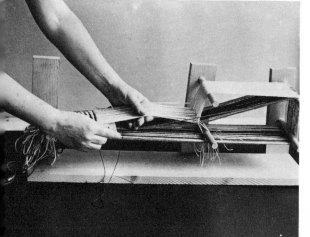

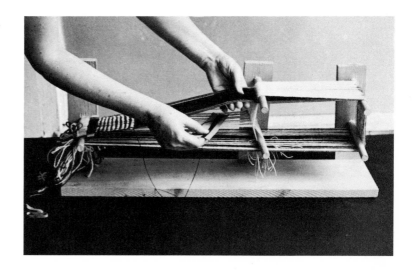

Fig. 102 Changing the shed:
raising the dark threads above
the white threads

finger of the other hand in the slightly opened shed and slide
your hand towards the second piece of cardboard. Carefully
place the weft thread half-way across the warp threads and
pull the end four inches down between the centre warp
threads. Change the shed. Always begin a new thread in the
centre of the warp. There should never be loose weft
threads at the selvedges unless it is intended as part of the
design. No knots are necessary. When the weft thread is
used up, drop a four-inch end centrally. Rewind the shuttle
and bring up the new thread alongside the one just dropped.
Pack or beat the threads down in the shed. Change the shed
between each shot of weft. At the conclusion of the weaving
pull the four-inch weft ends into the body of the work with
a crochet hook and snip closely.

As you near the second set of dowels and the shed opening
is small, it is time to move the warp around the loom.
Grasp the upper set of warps firmly in one hand and the
lower set in the other. Move the upper hand towards you
and the lower away from you so that the woven section
proceeds around and under the front dowel. When the bow
knots approach the upper bar of the second set of dowels
the weaving is completed. Untie the bows and slip the
heddles on to a safety-pin in readiness for the next piece.

Pick-up designs
Small designs, initial letters and other patterns can be
created by picking up individual threads from the lower
warp on a slender pointed stick, such as an hibachi stick.
When the lower warp is in the down position, these threads
from the lower warp can be woven into the upper warp.
Pattern designs will be clearest if two strongly contrasting

Above left
Fig. 103   Pick-up pattern using
   double threads in the spaces
Left
Fig. 104   Horizontal bars with the
   weft wrapping the warp
Above right
Fig. 105   Mexican fire dance
   figure: a combination of a thin
   and thick cotton thread

Fig. 106   Plying the fringe

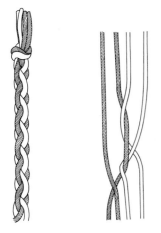

Fig. 107   Osage braid

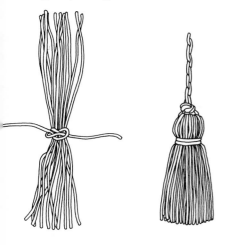

Fig. 108   Tassel

colours are used: one colour in the heddles and the other colour through the spaces. Try threading a combination of a thin yarn and a thick yarn to give the figured area added weight and dimension (fig. 105). In order to achieve a definite raised effect, thread each heddle with a single yarn and place two warp threads in the spaces between. The two threads in the spaces will work as one.

Finishing

A workable maximum width for the inkle loom is about five or six inches. Sometimes a greater width is desirable. Place the inkle bands side by side according to plan and join the pieces by carrying a needle threaded with a matching colour from selvedge to selvedge. Work flat, adjusting the tension so that the two pieces remain in alignment. Ends may be cut short and sewn together or they may be finished without fringe by drawing the warp threads back into the body of the work with a crochet hook.

Fringe variations may be simple or ornate. Wool fringe is easy to ply by hand because it is soft and fuzzy. Twist two groups of two or more strands tightly, holding a group in each hand, twisting in the same direction. Transfer both tightly held twisted groups to one hand and twist the two groups together in the reverse direction. Tie an overhand knot at the bottom (fig. 106). The woodland Indian braid, sometimes referred to as Osage braid, is worked with four strands in two contrasting colours (fig. 107). Select the strand on the right and pass it to the left behind the next two strands. Carry it over the third strand and return it to a position next to a strand of the same colour. The outside left-hand strand is worked next. Pass it behind two strands, to the right, bring it forward and over the strand of contrasting colour next to it and return it to its strand of the same colour on the left. Worked from either side the principle is: behind two strands and back over one strand. If the colours are alternated instead of paired the effect when the strands are tightened is tweedy and equally interesting. An overhand knot will secure the ends.

A tassel may be added before or after the overhand knot (fig. 108). Cut strands of yarn about $6\frac{1}{2}$ in. long for a 3 in. tassel. Tie a length of matching yarn in a square knot below the centre. Place the tassel strands on top of the fringe at the end of the piece of inkle weaving. Tie the ends of the fringe around the centre of the strands. Fold the top part of the tassel down over the bottom half until the ends are even. Warp wrap about $\frac{1}{2}$ in. down from the top with the same or a contrasting yarn or a thread of cotton or silk. The tassel can be very full or modest depending upon the number of pieces of yarn cut. An average tassel is composed of twelve to fifteen pieces.

The frame loom

The frame loom can be constructed in any size to fit any need (fig. 109). A travelling loom made to the exterior measurements of your suitcase and strapped to its side is acceptable in any baggage compartment. A portable frame loom, 24 × 36 in., is a comfortable arm's length and is easy to work sitting at a table. Clear pine or scrap wood free from knots may be used. You will need:

Two pieces of wood 1 × 2½ × 24 in. (for the frame)
Two pieces of wood 1 × 2½ × 36 in. (for the frame)
Four pieces of lath ⅛ × 1 × 25 in. (for shed sticks)
Small pieces of lath, 6, 8 and 12 in. long (for shuttles)
One ½ in. dowel 25 in. long (for a heddle bar)
Four 2 in. corner braces and sixteen screws
Small nails
1 in. headed nails

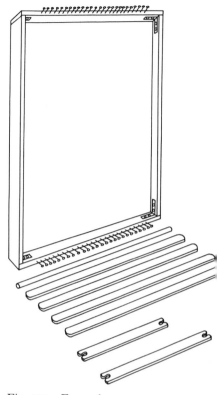

To assemble the frame, put some glue on the top of one of the 36 in. pieces of wood, set a 24 in. piece on top and secure it with two small nails; do the same with the other pieces and join them together as a frame. Then strengthen the inside corners with 2 in. corner braces. Turn upside down and finish the opposite side. Draw a pencil line down the centre of the narrow side of the 24 in. section. Starting 2½ in. from the end mark the line every ⅜ in., finishing 2½ in. from the end. Hammer a 1 in. headed nail about ⅜ in. down at each marked interval. The use of nails to separate the warp limits the weaving area to the front of the loom. Another way to separate the warp is with a coiled spring across the 24 in. section, or notching the sections with a file so that the warp can travel comfortably around the frame and provide extra length.

Fig. 109   Frame loom

One of the shed sticks is to be used as a sword stick, tapered and sanded on all sides. The small pieces of lath can be notched and sanded for shuttles. The shed sticks and the heddle bar rest on top of the frame.

Warping the loom

Warp directly on to the loom from a spool or ball of yarn, cord or twine. Choose a warp thread that will not break under tension and prolonged manipulation. A break can be repaired with a knot but it is a nuisance, so test the warp for strength. The type of warp thread is determined also by its visibility. For instance in traditional tapestry the warp is completely covered. Rug warp is also concealed and a strong smooth cotton or linen is necessary. The weaver must consider both colour and texture.

With the loom on a flat surface start the warp by wrapping

the thread a number of times around the bar, to the left and alongside the row of nails, across to the opposite side and around the second nail. Continue warping, ending at the opposite side; tie the warp thread around the bar, outside the last nail. There should be no slack, but the threads should not be stretched to the limit.

Inserting shed sticks
In order to stabilize the warp and increase the tension insert a shed stick under and over alternating threads. Begin with the first thread. The second stick is inserted under and over starting with the second thread, thereby effecting the first cross in the warp. Turn the second shed stick on end to open

Fig. 110 Woven wall-hanging by Melissa Cornfeld. Woven in three sections in blues, greens and purples of plain weave and Ghiordes knots

the shed and put in the third stick in the same shed as the second and push it up to the top of the frame. These three shed sticks remain in the loom while the weaving is in progress. The two sticks at the bottom of the loom provide a usable amount of warp for tying off the ends when the weaving is finished. Also, they maintain the tension and may be removed if the tension becomes too tight as the weaving progresses. The stick at the top moves up and down and when turned on end holds one shed open. The second shed is opened with the heddles attached to a heddle bar so that the alternate threads may be lifted in unison. Sometimes heddles are individual as they are on the inkle loom. Individual heddles work well for tapestry because the weaving proceeds on slightly different levels on short sections of the warp width. Individual heddles are also necessary on a very wide width because of the difficulty in controlling a very long heddle bar. The continuous heddle (fig. 111), attributed to the Navajo Indians, works well for up to about 36 in. As each heddle takes up about six inches of thread make a butterfly of a little more than six times the number of heddles needed. The heddles will open a second shed, controlling alternate threads.

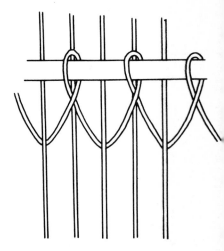

Fig. 111   Continuous heddle

Place the dowel across the frame over the warp threads. Tie the end of the butterfly around the dowel bar several times with a knot to hold it to the bar. From the right hand side take the butterfly under the first thread under the shed stick, over the heddle bar, around and through the opening to the right. Skip a thread, pick up the next thread under the shed stick with the butterfly, over the heddle bar and through the space to the right.

The heddles should be about $2\frac{1}{2}$ in. long. Hold the heddles on the bar about $2\frac{1}{2}$ in. above the warp and run the bar up and down to regulate the size of the heddles. The continuous heddle will adjust itself. Continue across and tie the end of the butterfly on to the bar with a few half hitches.

The fourth stick, called a sword stick, is inserted when the heddle bar is pulled up raising the alternate threads, thereby holding open the second shed. With the sword stick on end insert the first weft thread, allowing the end of the weft to drop between the centre warps.

Larger frames require stronger supports. A 5×7 ft frame should be made of 2×2 in. lumber. Any width larger than 7 ft is sturdier with a central support attached top and bottom with a flat iron brace.

A good sized portable frame of welded conduit tubing is self-standing. The hollow tubing allows for a simple tensioning device and storage space for the legs. You will need:

12 ft × 1 in. diameter electrical conduit tubing
6 ft × $\frac{3}{4}$ in. diameter electrical conduit tubing

Two $4\frac{1}{2} \times \frac{3}{4}$ in. diameter threaded rods
Two nuts for the above rods
Two $36 \times \frac{1}{2}$ in. diameter wooden dowels: one for a heddle bar the other cut in half—18 in. for the retractable third leg on the loom stand and the second 18 in. halved again and used as supports for the heddle bar
6 ft of rope (clothesline will do)
Three rubber caps for the legs.

Easy to assemble, the welding of the four joints and the two connections of the threaded rod can be inexpensively done at an automotive body repair shop. Rubber caps on the legs will protect the floor. The tensioning device essential for absolute tautness and gentle release of the warp makes the design of this loom ideal for tapestry weaving.

Weaving techniques and methods
Weave with the shed open, closed or with a combination of the two. Start with an inch of plain weave (tabby), using rug wool or roving to space and stabilize the warp. Traditional tapestry and rugs are often started with an inch of plain weave in linen or cotton matching the warp. Open the first shed by pulling down the top shed stick and turning it on end. Insert a flat shuttle wound with the filling thread, pull the shuttle through to the other side allowing the end of the thread to drop down about 4 in. between the centre warps. The second shed is opened by pulling up the heddle bar, inserting the sword stick and turning it on end. Return the shuttle through the newly opened shed to the other side, allowing the thread to form a wide arc. Break the arc into smaller arcs by pulling the weft towards you with the index finger. This is called bubbling. Beat with a comb. Change the shed again. The shed must be changed to form the cross that locks in the weft between each shot of weft. Always check the selvedges for straightness. The weft must be inserted loosely or the weaving will rapidly take on an hourglass shape. In a closely woven piece a thread can be run through this selvedge out to the frame, pulled taut and tied to the frame side.

The many possible arrangements of colour in the warp and weft provide infinite variety to a plain balanced weave. Try a warp of irregular stripes of different colours. An interesting effect occurs when two colours are wound on the shuttle at the same time.

The textures of different fibres also add variety. Try the laid-in technique to add unusual material. Along with the weft thread lay any fibre, unspun wool, paper, dried plant material or metal in the open shed. The laid-in material, if pliable, can be woven with the weft to form a design. Use a butterfly along with the shuttle weft.

Fig. 112   Tapestry loom of conduit tubing designed by Archie Brennan. The nut and threaded rod increase and release the tension of the warp

Fig. 113   Mexican back-strap loom: thin white cotton warp with multicoloured laid-in weft

Fig. 114   *Wall Number 1* (detail) Helen Frances Gregor. Tapestry weave, Ghiordes knots and laid-in anodized aluminium rods

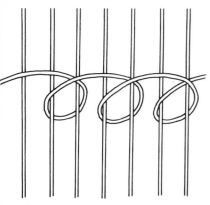

Fig. 115   Soumak stitch

Fig. 116   *Burning Seeds II* Tadek
Beutlich. Camel-hair, hand-dyed,
unspun jute, 84 × 72 in. Tapestry
weave, jute inserted in the
Soumak stitch
Photo John Artur

The Soumak stitch (fig. 115) adds a dimensional texture because when used in conjunction with plain weave it is raised in appearance. Soumak weaving is probably the oldest form of the Oriental rug. It is worked on a closed warp with butterflies: over four warp threads, down between the warp and back under two of the four warp threads, up and over four, down back and under two, etc. Soumak is very similar to back stitch or stem stitch in embroidery.

Specific designs can be woven from drawn pattern drafts using a pick-up stick. For instance, begin at the right selvedge, skip the first two threads, pick up four threads on a wide pick-up stick, skip two threads, pick up four, skip two, pick up four all the way across. Turn the pick-up stick on edge and insert a contrasting yarn. The contrasting yarn can stop there by cutting it from the butterfly and turning the loose end back around the next warp thread on the left

Fig. 117 Weaving from West Crete known as Kouskousse. Detail of a rising-bread cover, the loops formed around a bamboo stick across the warp, with wide borders of red griffins on a white ground. Woven at the turn of the century, probably in commemoration of Sir John Evans's discoveries at Knossos. Collection Mr and Mrs Leon Pomerance, New York

Fig. 118 *Award Yourself the CDM* Geraldine Brock. Pile of knots in wool, twine, worsted and linen in natural colours, 33 × 54 in. At the top, tapestry weave in purple, green, red, orange and blue
Photo Reg Cox

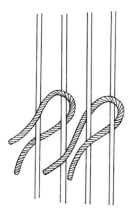

Fig. 119   Sehna knot

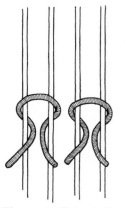

Fig. 120   Ghiordes knot

Fig. 121   Swedish knot with turn
at end of row

and bringing it back to the right for a few threads. The end will stay in when the weft is beaten down. Remove the pick-up stick and throw across the warp in the regular sheds one or two rows of plain weave. Close the shed and beat down. If the pattern continues from row to row the contrasting yarn on the butterfly can be carried up to the next row. This type of pattern will be geometric in appearance and can easily be worked out on graph paper so that the pick-ups are automatic.

Looping is similar to the pick-up pattern technique and is a very ancient form. Looping becomes a weft faced pile. Almost universal, it appears on Coptic tapestry as an embellishment, on many Peruvian textiles, and on those from Crete in the form known as Kouskousse (fig. 118). Looping is the basis of the contemporary Turkish towel. The loops are picked up with a knitting needle or on a pointed dowel stick. There should be two to four shots of tabby between rows of loops. Beat the tabby before the knitting needle is removed and after removal beat again to pack the loops tightly.

The knotted pile has many names, flossa, rya (of Scandinavian origin), Sehna (after a town in Iran) and Ghiordes, a town in Turkey. Flossa and rya knots are longer than the Ghiordes knot but are made in the same way. Sometimes Scandinavian rya rug techniques show one warp thread skipped between warps, but there is a basic difference in the length of the knot ends. An Oriental rug pile is worked around a gauge measuring stick about $\frac{3}{4}$ in. wide so that each knot has ends of equal size when cut across the groove in the gauge. In order to use a pile gauge stick (a piece of smoothly sanded narrow 1 in. lath works well), place it across the warp threads just above the last row of plain weave, extending about 1 or 2 in. beyond the desired area of knots. Ghiordes knots are tied from butterflies although the rows of plain weave may be carried on a shuttle. Always allow a selvedge of at least two warp threads at each end of the weaving. Work from right to left, or left to right if you prefer, but be consistent all the way through. Insert the butterfly under the third warp thread from the end on the left-hand side, over the top of the third and fourth warp, behind the fourth, the butterfly coming up between the third and fourth thread; bring the thread over, around and under the gauge stick, under the fifth warp from the left-hand side, over the top of the fifth and sixth warp, behind and under the sixth, coming up between the fifth and sixth warp and over and under the gauge stick. Repeat across the row. Turn the gauge stick on end and, with a sharp razor blade, cut the Ghiordes loops carefully down the centre of the length of the narrow side of the stick.

The Swedish knot (fig. 121) is a tapestry stitch in that it completely covers the warp, and is worked from the back,

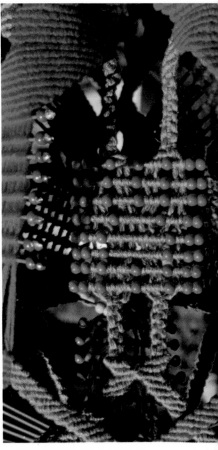

Fig. 123   *Masque 11* (detail)
Everett Sturgeon. Macramé
with dowels and beads

Fig. 122   *Masque 1* (detail)
Everett Sturgeon. Macramé
with dowels

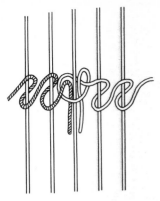

Fig. 124 Joining two colours in the Swedish knot

Fig. 125 Detail of Swedish knot covering single, double and triple warp threads, combined with plain weave

but it is entirely woven on a closed warp. Starting from the left on the reverse side, slide the butterfly behind the first warp, wrap the tail in a loop around the warp, bring it over the top and pull through the centre space; pull down on the right side of the warp. Bring the butterfly bobbin over, around, under and over the next warp thread. To turn a corner bring the butterfly over the last warp around in a loop, emerging from behind the warp in the space formed by the loop. Continue towards the left, reversing all the stitches. It requires some experience to know how tight to pull the weft. If the warp is widely spaced each knot will be widely spaced; pull the weft tighter and the position of the warps will be distorted. This distortion is one of the most interesting aspects of the stitch. Use a group of warp threads as a single unit and the thickness of the knot will be changed. Openings, slits and silhouette shapes are also possible.

Gauze weaves

The delicate beauty of lacy weaves is intriguing. Perhaps there is a quality of mystery inherent in transparent shadowy open work made by crossing the warp threads. The terms gauze and leno are used interchangeably although leno appears to refer to a type of Indian heddle in which the warp threads are twisted with the opening of the alternate shed. Some of the more complicated design arrangements are called Mexican and Spanish lace although a good many are of Guatemalan and Peruvian origin.

Provision must be made for extra warp because the gauze weave process of crossing and recrossing uses it up rapidly. The best way is to suspend the warp from the frame on a loom stick as described in the section on twining (page 23). Change the distance between the loom stick and the frame as the tension tightens. On the loom built of conduit tubing the tensioning device can be expanded to its fullest before starting the warp winding. The frame loom should be warped loosely and the thickness of the shed sticks increased by taping a few layers of newspaper around them. Another solution would be to add to the height of the shed sticks with some long narrow blocks of wood. Remove the extenders as the warp tightens, then remove the first shed stick at the bottom and the second stick when necessary.

Always start the gauze weave on the right-hand side with the first right warp up or in the open shed.

A flat stick under odd numbered warp threads makes it easier to keep track of the correct warp threads to pick up and drop.

A generous amount of plain weave is necessary on the edges as well as across the warp to keep the warp from pulling towards the centre in an hourglass shape.

*

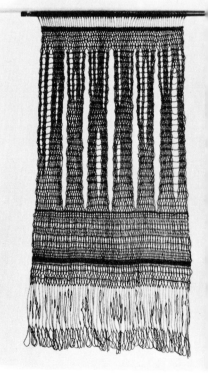

Fig. 126 *White Satellite* Shirley Marein. Woven on a frame loom, Swedish knot and twining, 96 × 108 in.

Fig. 127 *Gauze 2* May Gower. Gauze weave with wrapped warp in dark brown horsehair and light brown wool, 36 × 68 in. Photo Mark Gerson

Simple gauze weave

The simple gauze weave (fig. 128) is a 1/1 twist, usually called leno.

a four rows of plain weave.

b starting on the right, with the left hand pick up warp 1, pull slightly to the left.

c with the right hand, pick up warp 2, pull up and to the right, over warp 1.

d slip the weft, wound on a shuttle, under warp 2 and repeat steps b and c across the warp. Another method is to slip a narrow shed stick under warp 2, repeat across the row. After the row is complete, turn the shed stick on end and insert any supplementary weft such as raffia, a reed or a metal rod.

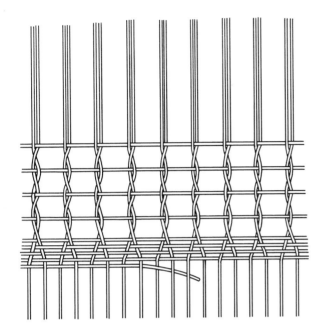
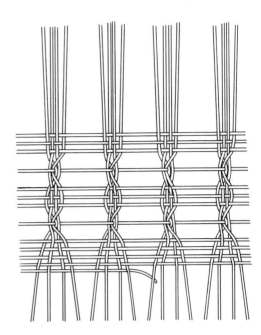

Fig. 128   Simple gauze weave

Fig. 129   Pick up two, drop two

Gauze and plain weave combination
Alternating plain weave with 1/1 twist can make any repeat design form.
a   six rows of plain weave.
b   starting on the right, twist warp 1 with warp 2, warp 3 with warp 4; then plain weave warp 5 through warp 10, twist warp 11 with warp 12 and warp 13 with warp 14; plain weave across 15 through 20, twist 21 with 22, 23 with 24; plain weave, etc. Repeat this sequence three times.
c   in the next sequence alternate the plain weave with the gauze twist.

Pick up two, drop two (fig. 129)
a   four rows of plain weave starting on the left.
b   starting on the right, with the left hand pick up warps 1 and 3, pulling to the left.
c   pick up warps 2 and 4 on a pick-up stick. Put stick over and past warps 1 and 3.
d   with the left hand pull warps 5 and 7 to the left. Pick up warps 6 and 8 on the pick-up stick and put stick over and past warps 5 and 7.
e   continue to the end of the warp, pulling the weft through after the pick-up stick.
f   from the left-hand side, put the pick-up stick under all even warp threads and pull the weft back to the right.

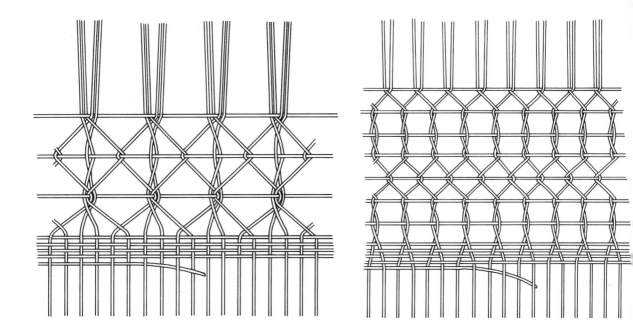

Single twist, alternating warp (fig. 130)
a   four rows of plain weave starting on the left-hand side.
b   pick up one, drop one acorss the row. Insert the tabby from left to right.
c   place a flat stick under all uneven warp threads. Pull the warp 1 to the left, pick up warps 2 and 4 from under the flat stick on a pick-up stick and pass over warp 1. Continue across row, picking up one cord dropping one cord.
d   a larger, more open type of twist can be created by pulling warp 3 to the left, picking up warp 6 and passing it over warp 3. Continue this sequence to the end of the row. At the end, warp 24, let us say, will pass over 21 and 23 in order to make up for the two used at the start.

2/2 twist, alternating warp (fig. 131)
a   four rows of plain weave.
b   drop two warp threads (warps 1 and 3), pick up three for the first cross, then drop two and pick up two the rest of the way across. At the right side there will be extra top warps to be dropped and passed over. Use the flat stick to help.
c   insert the tabby from left to right.
d   alternating row, pick up one, drop one.

Elaborate 2/2 twist, alternating warp (fig. 132)
a   four rows of plain weave.
b   first gauze row: pick up two and drop two across the row. Insert tabby from left to right.
c   second gauze row: pick up one, drop one, continue across row. Tabby from right to left.

Fig. 130   Single twist, alternating warp

Fig. 131   2/2 twist, alternating warp

74

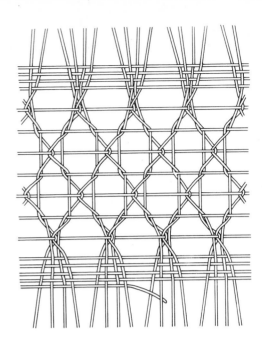

Fig. 132   Elaborate 2/2 twist,
alternating warp

d   third gauze row: pick up one, drop one, then pick up
     two, drop two and continue across picking up two and
     dropping two. Insert tabby from left to right.
e   after seven rows of gauze weave, insert four rows of plain
     weave. Repeat rows of gauze weave. The rows of plain
     weave may be deeper if desired.

Regular and opposite twist
a   four rows of plain weave.
b   pick up one, drop one across the row. Insert tabby from
     left to right.
c   pull warps 1 and 3 to the right. Slip pick-up stick under
     warp 2 and bring it up to the left of warps 1 and 3.
d   pull warp 5 to the right and pick up warp 4 at the left of
     warp 5. Proceed across, pick up one, drop one. At the left
     side the last two even warps work together as one.
e   repeat rows b and c.

Right and left 2/2 twist
In this weave the weft must be pulled tight to show the
twist.
a   four rows of plain weave.
b   first gauze row: pull warps 1 and 3 to the left. Pick up
     warps 2 and 4 on pick-up stick and pass stick over threads
     1 and 3. Continue across lifting all even warps. Insert
     tabby from left to right.
c   second gauze row: pull warps 1, 3, 5, 7 to the right, slip
     pick-up stick under threads 2 and 4 and bring stick up to
     the left of 1, 3, 5, 7. Pull 9 and 11 to right, slip pick-up

75

stick under 6 and 8 and bring up to the left of 9 and 11. Proceed across, picking up two and dropping two.

(c) second gauze row (alternative): pull warps 1, 3, 5 to the right, slip pick-up stick under threads 2 and 4 and bring stick up to the left of threads 1, 3 and 5. Pull 7 and 9 to the right and slip stick under 6 and 8 and bring up to the left. Proceed across, picking up two and dropping two.

d   repeat row b.

Simple, fast, no-shed, gauze weave
This gauze weave requires a great deal of tabby to hold it in place, otherwise it has a tendency to slide about.

a   four rows of plain weave, beginning from right to left.
b   first gauze row (1/1 twist): start on the right and pull warp 1 to the left, slide pick-up stick under warp 2 and slip stick over warp 1. Pull warp 3 to the left, pick up warp 4 with pick-up stick and pass stick over warp 3. Continue across.
c   five rows of plain weave.
d   second gauze row (2/2 twist): pull warps 1 and 2 to the left, place pick-up stick under warps 3 and 4, pass stick over warps 1 and 2. Pull warps 5 and 6 to the left, place the pick-up stick under warps 7 and 8 and pass the stick over 5 and 6. Continue across the warp.
c   five rows of plain weave.
d   third gauze row (3/3 twist): pull warps 1, 2 and 3 to the right, pick up 4, 5 and 6; pass stick over 1, 2 and 3, etc. Continue as above.

Simple warp wrap gauze weave, no shed
This weave also requires a great deal of plain weave to hold it in place and it is advisable to use the plain weave generously on the sides. The number of warp threads in each group will produce a different effect and depends, to some extent, on the dividing of the groups into the total number of warp threads. Take care that there are not too many or too few threads over at the end.

a   six rows of plain weave, starting on the right.
b   first wrapped row: slip weft thread under first four warps and bring the weft up between warps 4 and 5. Carry the weft around the four warps to the right, under and across the back of 5, 6, 7 and 8. After pulling the weft tight around the first four warps, bring the weft up between threads 8 and 9, around 5, 6, 7 and 8 to the right, under and across the back to 9, 10, 11 and 12. Continue across the warp.
c   insert next row of tabby from left to right. Plain weave for three rows.
d   second wrapped row: repeat as above.
e   four rows of plain weave.

Next, either repeat steps b, c, d and e or continue as follows:

f   four rows of plain weave.

g   third wrapped row: wrap warps 1 and 2, then 3, 4, 5 and 6, continue across in groups of four, wrapping the last two as the first two.

h   one row of plain weave from left to right.

i   fourth wrapped row: wrap 1, 2, 3 and 4. Continue across in groups of four.

j   one row of plain weave from left to right.

k   fifth wrapped row: same as third wrapped row.

l   five rows of plain weave.

Another effect can be achieved using the same procedure as above but with three rows of plain weave between wrapped rows.

Wrapped groups of warps with shed (bouquet pattern) (fig. 133)

The odd numbered warps form the upper shed and in the lower shed are the even numbered warps. Place a flat stick under all odd numbered warps (i.e. over all even numbered warps).

a   four rows of plain weave.

b   the same group of warps are wrapped together in each row of wrapped warps. Starting on the right, pass the weft under the first three odd numbered warps 1, 3, 5; bring weft up between threads 5 and 7, carry it back over 1, 3, 5 and enter in shed again; bring under 1, 3, 5, pull; pass weft under 7, 9, 11; bring weft up between 11 and 13, pass back over 7, 9, 11, then under 7, 9, 11 again, pull; then under 13, 15, 17, etc.

c   any number of warps may be wrapped, odd or even, but there should always be an odd number of rows of plain weave so that the wrapping always starts from the right-hand side: therefore, three rows of plain weave. Repeat rows of wrapped warps.

Alternating shed (diamond bouquet) (fig. 133)

This particular pattern requires an even number of rows of plain weave and an odd number of warps to be wrapped. Again the upper shed is made up of the odd numbered warps and the lower shed of the even numbered warps. Place a flat stick under all odd numbered warps.

a   seven rows of plain weave.

b   first row of wrapped warps: starting on the left-hand side, wrap the first three odd numbered warps, then proceed as for step b above (bouquet pattern).

c   two rows of plain weave.

d   second row of wrapped warps: starting on the left, the warp that was left unwrapped in the previous row is now in the centre of the warps to be wrapped and they are

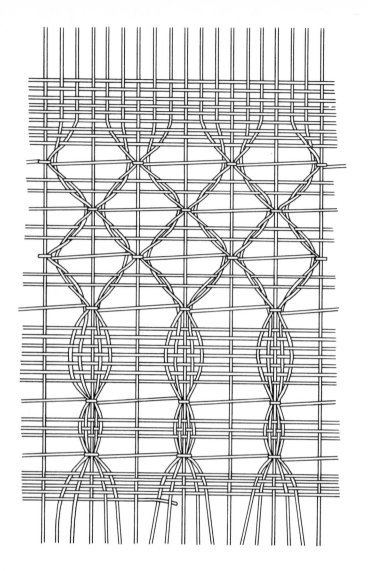

Fig. 133 Wrapped groups of warps
with shed (bouquet pattern) and
alternating shed (diamond
bouquet)

picked up from under the stick. These are even numbered.
Slip the weft under the last warp on the left, let us say 24,
22, 20, 18, 16; wrap around 20, 18, 16; then proceed to
the right and wrap around 14, 12, 10, then 8, 6, 4, etc.
e   two rows of plain weave.
f   third row of wrapped warps: start on the right with the
odd numbered warps in the up position. Proceed as step d
above.

Rug making techniques

Some rugs are plain weave, some have a pile and some have
a combination of both; all are made of sturdy materials and
have a common purpose. The tapestry technique, essen-
tially plain weave, is the technique used in the most
exquisite Flemish tapestry and the most rugged Navajo

Indian floor covering. The pile rug is known all over the world. Early Germanic tribes devised a rough fabric in imitation of animal fur for warmth. The looped pile used in areas as far apart as Crete, Egypt and Peru had many uses: as protection from the abrasiveness of harnesses, necessary for carrying burdens; for warmth; for protection from the elements; for the bed; for the table; for the floor; and for decoration. The knotted pile, looped or cut, is the most long wearing, the knot holding the loop firmly in place, the pile receiving the wear.

The Ghiordes knot (fig. 120) is common to many Oriental, European and American rugs. It is formed around two adjacent warp threads. The centre of a piece of yarn is placed across the two warp threads, the cut ends of the piece of yarn are wrapped around the warp threads, emerging between them. Grasp the cut ends and pull down. The length of the piece of yarn used to tie the knot may be any size from about 2 to 6 in. Persian rugs have a uniform short pile and Chinese rugs a sculptured pile, the design outlined with a groove carved in the pile; the Scandinavian rya rugs have a longer flowing pile. All are simply constructed by alternating four or five rows of plain weave with one row of Ghiordes knots.

The knotted rug can be made on a frame loom in sections as small as a foot square and assembled by whipping the sections together; or if you prefer it can be made on a very large frame. On the other hand if you enjoy working on a large surface spread out before you like a canvas, warp the entire rug right on the wall of your room from the floor or baseboard to the ceiling (fig. 135). It is a good idea to nail strips of wood, blocked out from the wall top and bottom, if the mouldings are very flat or there are none at all. About three inches of space between the wall and the warp threads is needed for the movement of the hands and the expansion of the warp as it is filled. The warp can either be attached to a loom bar and suspended from hooks or nails, top and bottom, so that the tension can be released, or a series of nails can be inserted top and bottom and the warp wound directly around them.

Wind the warp even but loose, take up the slack with tightly folded newspapers as well as with shed sticks, removing the papers as necessary to release the tension. If the warp is wide tie the heddles individually rather than continuously. Before starting, twine across the warp at the bottom to spread the warp evenly.

Start and finish, top and bottom, with at least an inch of plain weave. Between rows plain weave may be from $\frac{1}{2}$ to 1 in. depending on the length of the knots. Longer knots cover more of the plain weave.

Draw a chalk line on the wall or tie a cord from top to

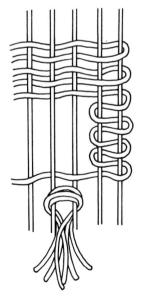

Fig. 134 Detail of selvedge, plain weave and Ghiordes knots

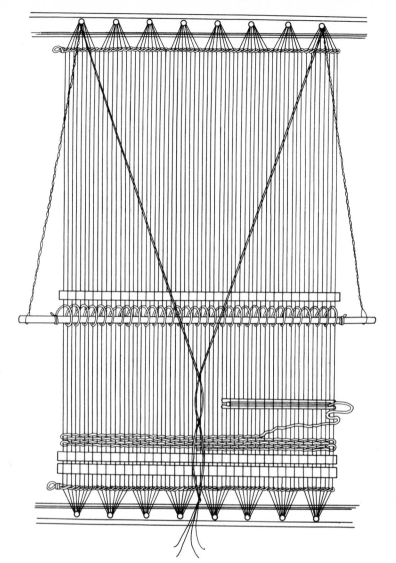

Fig. 135   Warping a rug

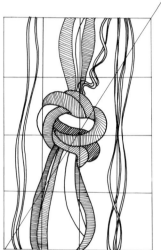

Fig. 136   Sketch for a rug design
with a grid for scaling to size

bottom as a guide to keeping the sides at right angles to the
bottom.

The selvedge may be two or four warp threads at both
sides of the width, depending upon the length of the knot.
The purpose of the selvedge is to keep the edges of the rug
from curling under. The selvedge requires more plain weave
than the areas between knots. As you weave keep the
selvedges abreast of the knotted rows.

If you work from a colour sketch draw it to scale. For
instance, if your finished rug is to be 4×6 ft, you could
quarter the size for convenience: $1 \times 1\frac{1}{2}$ ft is about right for
clarity. Too small a sketch is deceptive and difficult to render
in colour. Use coloured pencils, crayons, watercolours or a
combination. The sketch can be interpreted accurately by

drawing and colouring it on graph paper. Each square, starting at the left and numbered horizontally across the bottom, represents each knot. Numbered consecutively, a rug four feet wide, eight ends to the inch, will have four knots every inch or a total of 192 knots. Although each square on the graph paper is small it is less cumbersome if each square represents two knots for a total of 96 squares. Each square numbered and running vertically from the bottom up the left-hand side represents each row of knots plus the plain weave.

A free interpretation can be made by drawing a grid in pencil on top of the coloured sketch (fig. 136). First divide the sketch in quarters, then quarter each quarter so the sketch is divided into sixteenths. Make the same grid on the warp strings with a felt tip pen or coloured paint. Draw the section of the design that appears in each square on the warp threads with coloured markers or tempera paint.

Determining the amount of warp and weft for a rug
Use a strong plied linen or cotton cord for the warp. An 8/5 natural coloured linen warp is suitable (8/5 means that five strands, each strand composed of eight single threads, is plied or twisted together for strength and weight). The quantity needed is calculated by multiplying the number of warp threads per inch by the width in inches by the length in inches. Convert to yardage. Most cotton and linen is sold by the yardage per pound. Most rug designs can be expressed in three or four knots per inch. Remember that it takes two warp ends to make a Ghiordes knot, so three knots would require six ends of warp per inch, four knots eight ends of warp per inch.

The amount of weft required can vary from $\frac{1}{2}$ lb. to 1 lb. per square foot according to the length of the knots. Width multiplied by length equals the square footage. A rug 4 × 6 ft contains 24 square feet and, if extravagantly woven, 24 lb. of wool. About a quarter of this amount is for plain weave filling and selvedges. An easy way to work out how much of each colour is needed is to list the colours on a piece of paper according to hue; for instance: olive green, emerald green, light green and dark green in one group; red, orange, maroon, pink and scarlet in another; and turquoise, prussian blue and ultramarine in a third group. All colours that function in the same chromatic group make a certain percentage of the total, so that, for instance, the green group, red group and blue group each make up a third of the total. After subtracting the wool needed for the plain weave and selvedges, a third of the remaining 18 lb. for each group of colours equals 6 lb. each. The amounts can be broken down further within each group.

Rya rugs are often made from a 2-ply wool or cowhair,

137 Pile rug by Peter Collingwood

in many hues of close tonal value. Try a variety of yarns in each knot; a smooth surfaced yarn with a fuzzy one; every so often a very thin thread or a silky one. Cut two different lengths of yarn to be used together for extra variety. The lengths of the knot threads can vary up to an inch. Prepare two templates of $\frac{1}{2}$ in. pressed composition board, $4\frac{1}{2}$ in. square and $5\frac{1}{2}$ in. square for cutting yarn for the knots. Wind the yarn round and round these squares, no more than $\frac{1}{2}$ in. thick on each side, secure top and bottom with rubber bands and cut firmly across the narrow edges with a single-edged razor blade. Store the cut pieces in plastic bags or small boxes. Keep them around you as a palette from which to choose the colour and texture for each knot.

Contemporary wall-hangings

Tapestry weaves

Tapestry techniques have undergone revolutionary changes. Classic tapestry, because of its exacting nature and great cost, is rare in some countries and is rapidly disappearing in others. Tapestry traditionally designed by an artist and worked by artisans has given way to a new form—the artist craftsman designing and working directly with his medium.

Tapestry can be woven on almost any type of loom. The weave is plain, the weft completely covering the warp. The warp, strong and evenly taut, generally consists of ten ends to the inch. After warping, insert the shed sticks. There are several ways to apply the heddles. Using strong cotton cord, cut 15 in. lengths for single heddles. There are half as many heddles needed as there are warp threads. Encircle the even warp threads from under the shed stick with a single heddle cord, wrap the cut end around the heddle bar and tie in front of the bar with a square knot. A stationary rest for the heddle bar will free the hands for the manipulation of the bobbins necessary for the various colour changing techniques. Attach a 3 in. L-shaped corner brace to both sides of the frame to hold the heddle bar. Place the holders about 5 in. down from the top of the frame. Should the bar tend to roll off the braces twist a few rubber bands around the end of the protruding section of the brace. A C clamp screwed to the edges of the frame, or a grooved piece of composition board attached to the frame, will also hold the heddle bar. Try a continuous heddle with half hitches to space the heddles and hold them firmly in place (fig. 139). Place the heddle cord under the warp thread to be raised, over the heddle bar and half hitch to the right; then make another hitch to the left, tighten the hitches and make two more; then, over the top of the bar again and pick up the next warp thread.

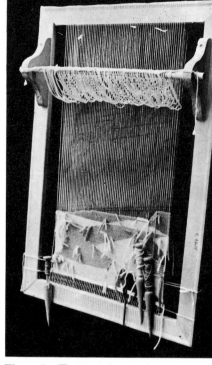

Fig. 138   Tapestry loom of canvas stretchers as suggested by Mary Black, ideal for small pieces (artist's canvas stretchers tend to warp under tension in sizes over 18 × 24 in.). Weaving by Rosalie Adolf

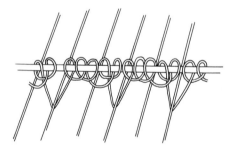

Fig. 139   Tapestry heddles with half hitches for spacing

Fig. 140   *My Victorian Aunt* Archie Brennan. Cotton warp, wool, cotton and metal weft, 78 × 55 in. Tapestry technique. Property of Michael Laird ARIBA, Edinburgh
Photo Tom Scott

MY VICTORIAN AUNT
WHO REALLY KNEW A
THING OR TWO

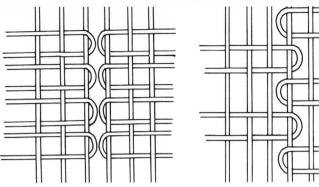

Fig. 141 Vertical slit Fig. 142 Vertical dovetail Fig. 143 Vertical interlocking

Tapestry weaving is worked in different sections that progress independently. Rarely is the shed opened and the shuttles passed through in a straight line; therefore, the shed need only be opened a section at a time. Insert the weft loosely under small sections of the warp, press down with a finger or the point of the tapestry bobbin, in small arcs; beat into position and go forward another few inches. Tapestry is woven from the back, ends are left hanging and held in place by beating down the weft. Start with about two inches of plain weave in the same material as the warp, turn under for a flush finish. In order to be able to slip in a rod for hanging, finish with plain weave of the same warp material so that it can be turned back and hemmed.

Vertical slit (fig. 141)
Two weft threads of different colours, coming towards each other, turn back to form a straight line and a slit between colours. The slit can be whipped together with matching, very fine invisible thread upon completion of the work. The open slit becomes a strong design element when exaggerated in length and of any width, in one colour or multicoloured.

Vertical dovetailing (fig. 142)
Two weft threads of different colours come towards each other turn back around the same warp thread, one above the other leaving no slit. The edge is textured.

Vertical interlocking (fig. 143)
Two weft threads of the same or different colours, coming towards each other meet between warps, turn around each other and return in the direction from which they came. For a smooth joining keep the threads in order, looping in the same direction. In a single colour, capricious joining can result in an interesting textural ridge.

Fig. 144 Detail of tapestry weaving showing various techniques for joining different colours. The design is drawn on the warp

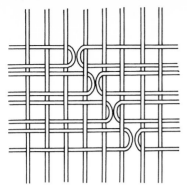

Fig. 145   Diagonal slit

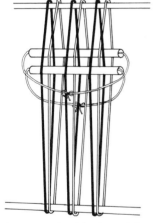

Fig. 146   Positioning of the cylinders in double weaving

Diagonal slit (fig. 145)
Two weft threads of different colours coming towards each other from opposite directions turn back in the same manner as the vertical slit technique. But in each successive row the turning back occurs one warp thread ahead, or one warp thread back according to the direction of the slant desired. Dovetailing and interlocking can also occur on the diagonal.

Combine the tapestry technique with knotting, netting, wrapping, soumak, embroidery as well as combining different materials. Explore and elaborate on the slit technique. Try a dimensional tapestry, a new silhouette or assemble a series of woven pieces into a collage.

Double weaving
Double weaving is tricky but it is worth trying. It is simply two sets of warp threads, one placed over the other, woven one at a time, with one thread going round and round making a tube, or two weft threads shuttling from left to right and right to left connecting on one side or the other. Each set of warp threads has its own set of sheds.

Woven in plain weave the rear warp makes an excellent background for a gauze weave on the face warp. Two strongly contrasting colours are suitable for the gauze weave or a pick-up design. Avoid fuzzy yarns that have a tendency to stick to each other. Start with a piece of modest width. Set the warp threads close together so that the weaving will be warp faced and the weft hidden. For a two-colour warp wind the two colours together, alternating a warp thread of one colour with a warp thread of the other colour, one colour alongside the other.

Use two $1\frac{1}{2}$ in. cylinders of cardboard (the kind that hold wax paper or aluminium foil) to separate the sheds (fig. 146). Place one cylinder behind all the warp threads of one colour plus the alternate or the odd numbered threads of the second colour. Slip a long cord through the hollow of the cylinder and tie in front of the warp. The other cylinder is placed behind the alternate or even threads of the second colour, the cord passed through the cylinder and tied in the *back* of all the warp threads. The second cylinder duplicates the position of the first cylinder, but in reverse, both acting as shed sticks. The other sheds are opened with a continuous heddle on a heddle bar. The front heddles pull up and the back heddles pull down. Contrasting colours can exchange places. Bring the colour at the rear to the front, a pair at a time with a wide pick-up stick, turning it on edge to serve as a shed stick.

Double weaving requires a great deal of patience. A pick-up design is painstaking, whether on a backstrap, frame or multi-harness loom. Double, triple and even quadruple

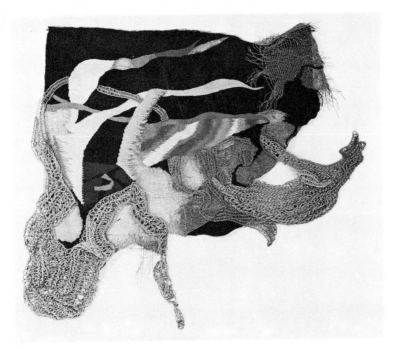

Fig. 147 *Reaching Out* Betsey Bess.
Tapestry with looped needle
netting of wool, twine and rope

Fig. 148 *Camel* Fiona Mathison.
Warp of cowhair, weft of
cowhair and wool, 72 × 96 in.
Tapestry technique

Fig. 149 *From Her Tower—
Whilst Half Awake He Answers*
Maureen Hodge. Tapestry weave
with macramé of wool and linen
on cotton warp.
Property of the Scottish Arts
Council

Fig. 150 Wall-hanging by Melissa
Cornfeld. Slit technique, plain
weave
Photo Michael Cornfeld

Fig. 151 *Mask* Sally Sankus.
Plain weave of raffia, woven
directly on the frame

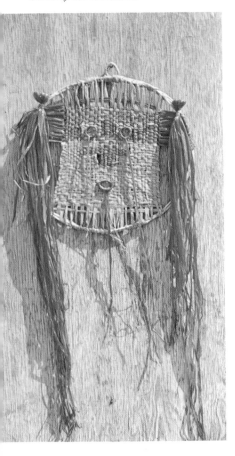

weaving is well known among primitive peoples who devised the method out of necessity for widths wider than the back-strap could comfortably support, in addition to tubular cording and strong banding of double cloth. With a little ingenuity layered weaving adds depth and dimension.

Looped warp

An unusual warp faced weave, well known to the ancient Peruvians, is the discontinuous interlocked warp. The warp descends a certain distance, loops around another warp thread and returns (fig. 153). It is rather like a linear patchwork using many colours and textures. Tie or nail guide cords to the sides of the frame according to the desired break up of the warp threads. Use these cords to hold the loops of warp so that the next coloured warp can loop around the one above it (fig. 154). Remove the guide cords before weaving. Near the loop areas you will probably have to insert the weft with a needle. If you can loop once you can in principle loop any number of times, creating many layers from different points, emanating from the interior of the frame from any created negative space.

Fig. 152 *Pilgrim* Lenore Tawney. Double-weave hanging in black and white with 14K gold stripes, 16 × 69 in.
From the J. Walter Thompson Company Art Collection

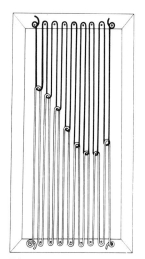

Fig. 153

Fig. 154

Far left
Fig. 153 Basic two-colour interlocked warp thread

Left
Fig. 154 Interlocking warp of many colours. Supplementary thick, taut guide cords are necessary, functioning as loom bars

Tie dyeing the warp

The tie dyeing of warp threads before weaving in order to produce a design or pattern is known as 'ikat'. The method involves either controlling the dye so that it will penetrate the threads in selected areas or the bleaching out of previously dyed yarns. Both warp and weft threads may be dyed, caused to resist the dye or to discharge the dye—but dyeing the warp to form a pattern and allowing the weft to be of a uniform colour is simpler. There are an infinite number of possibilities for designing.

Precut the warp threads to fit the loom, allowing at least 18 in. for the resist knotting and for fitting and tying on the loom.

If you have a plan for a design prepare it in cut paper, crayons or paints.

Carefully lay the warp threads over the design area. Mark or tie the threads in small groups to designate the areas that are to resist the dye (fig. 156). Number the groups of warp threads so that after the dyeing they can be put on the loom in order.

Wrap the resist areas (fig. 157). There are many methods and materials to use: rubber bands, waxed threads, saran wrap, fibre-glass, polyethylene and other synthetic materials resistant to dye. Knotting and a combination of knotting and wrapping will produce different textural effects.

Fragmentation of the design is less likely if a warp faced weaving is planned. A thick dense warp woven with a fine weft thread is preferable, although the possibilities are endless.

A weaver who is not inventive is a competent but limited artisan. Create on a circular frame, a triangular frame or on an asymmetrical construction. Place warp threads in the

Fig. 155 *Strata* Louise Todd. Interlocked warp of wool; each section of warp is interlocked with another colour of warp, 16 × 42 in.

Fig. 156 Warp threads tied in groups over a design for tie dyeing

Fig. 157 Tie dyeing the warp: here the warp is tied with waxed marine string and the top is covered with plastic wrap

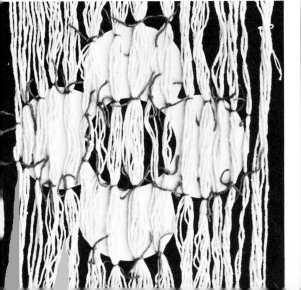

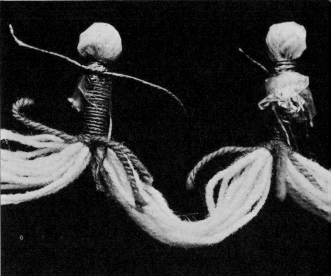

Fig. 158 *Growth* Myriam Gilby. Horsehair, jute, wool, rags, metal washers, twine, etc. woven on a frame loom with a great deal of finger weaving, soumak and warp wrapping, height 84 in.

Fig. 159 *Eskimo Pie* Shirley Marein. Double weaving of unspun wool, plyed wool and feathers, 12 × 24 in.

shape of the letter Y, attenuating, reshaping and devising new forms.

Mount wall-hangings very simply on a wooden or metal rod. Avoid pretentious framing. Allow the hanging an importance of its own and maintain the natural integrity of the materials.

Acknowledgements

No book springs into bloom spontaneously. Years of study, practice and teaching precede the actual production of the book; however, certain early pivotal relationships pave the way, sometimes without the knowledge of the people involved. To these people I am deeply indebted. Many years ago Melissa Cornfeld inadvertently introduced me to the inkle and frame looms, providing basic designs for the diagrams in this book. Over the years she has continued to share her studies, experience and expertise. A special tribute is due to Edith Karlin who undertook the difficult task of constructing and detailing the examples of gauze weave. My heart-felt thanks to Janet Silberstein whose generosity, devotion and craftsmanship were of inestimable help in working some of the examples in this book.

Curt Meinel has my deepest gratitude for his advice and consultation on the photography. I am most grateful to Eleanor Bello for the superb styling of most of the renderings.

Many thanks to all people, near and far, who thoughtfully shared their work and knowledge with me in person and through correspondence: Rosalie Adolf, Marie Aiken, Betsey Bess, Archie Brennan, Peter Collingwood, Michael Cornfeld, Yvonne Forbath, Myriam Gilby, Betty Goldberg, Esther Gotthoffer, Robert Griemsmann, David Holborne, Norma Kershaw, Robert Mabon, Harriet Pomerance, Sally Sankus, Isolde Savage, Marjorie Snow, Milton Sonday, Everett Sturgeon, Louise Todd and many, many others.

Sources of supply

European suppliers

Craftsman's Mark Ltd, 36 Shoreheath Road, Farnham, Surrey, England (natural coloured wools)

CUM Textile Industries, 5 Rosemersgade, 1362 Copenhagen K, Denmark (rug wool, cowhair, linen)

Dryad Handicrafts, Northgates, Leicester, England (wool, cotton, looms)

The Hand Loom Weavers, Fourways, Rockford, Ringwood, Hampshire, England (cotton, wools)

Harriss Looms, North Grove Road, Hawkhurst, Kent, England (looms, accessories)

J. Hyslop Bathgate and Co., Island Street, Galashiels, Scotland (wools)

Stavros Kouyoumoutzakis, Kalokerinov Avenue 166, Iraklion, Crete, Greece (natural colour homespun)

The Multiple Fabric Co. Ltd, Dudley Hill, Bradford 4, England (horsehair, belting yarn, white wool, mohair)

Joseph Skilbeck Bros Ltd, 55 Glengall Road, London, SE15 (chemicals and dyes)

North American suppliers

City Chemical Corporation, 132 West 22nd Street, New York, NY 10011, USA (mordants, dyes)

William Condon & Sons Ltd, 65 Queen Street, Charlottetown, PO Box 129, Prince Edward Island, Canada (wools)

Empire Twine and Yarn, 7 Caesar Place, Moonachie, New Jersey 07074, USA (jute, cotton cord)

Frederick J. Fawcett Inc., 129 South Street, Boston, Massachusetts 02111, USA (natural and coloured linens)

Fiber Yarn Co. Inc., 840 Sixth Avenue, New York, NY 10001, USA (macramé cording, raffia, novelty)

Filature Lemieux Inc., St Ephren Cte, Beauce, Quebec, Canada (wool)

Golden Fleece Woolens, Box 123, Agincourt, Ontario, Canada (raw wool, greased or scoured)

Greentree Ranch, Rte. 3 Box 461, Loveland, Colorado 80537, USA (raw wool and alpaca fleece)

Keystone Aniline & Chemical Inc., 321 North Loomis Street, Chicago, Illinois 60609, USA (dyes)

Lily Mills Co, Dept HWH, Shelby, North Carolina 28150, USA (cotton, linen, jute, wool)

The Mannings, R.D. 2 East Berlin, Pennsylvania 17316, USA (rug wool)

Mexiskein, PO Box 1624, Missoula, Montana 59801, USA (handspun Mexican wool)

Paternayan Brothers Inc., 312 East 95th Street, New York, NY 10028, USA (rug wool and backing, tapestry and crewel wool)

School Products, 312 East 23rd Street, New York, NY 10010, USA (looms, wool, accessories)

The Yarn Depot, 545 Sutter Street, San Francisco, California 94102, USA (rug wool, cotton, novelty)

Australian suppliers

Guild Yarn Shop (Hand Weavers and Spinners Guild of Australia, members only), Box 67 GPO Sydney, New South Wales 2001 (all yarns)

Spinners and Weavers Suppliers, PO Box 186, Double Bay, New South Wales 2028 (all yarns and equipment)

Grazcos, c/o Mrs Jenkins, 9 Bent Street, Lindfield, New South Wales 2070 (fleece)

Wondoflex Yarn Crafts, 1 Rose Street, Gardenvale, Victoria 3185 (wool, cotton, linen)

Bibliography

Ashley, Clifford W. *The Book of Knots*. London: Faber
and Faber; New York: Doubleday and Co. Inc., 1944
Atwater, Mary Meigs *Byways in Handweaving*. London
and New York: Macmillan Co., 1954
Birrell, Verla *The Textile Arts*. London and New York:
Harper and Row, 1959
Black, Mary E. *New Key to Weaving*. Milwaukee: Bruce
Publishing Co., 1957
D'Harcourt, Raoul *Textiles of Ancient Peru and their
Techniques*. Seattle: University of Washington Press, 1962
De Dillmont, Theresa *Encyclopedia of Needlework*.
Mulhouse, France: DMC Library
Emery, Irene *The Primary Structures of Fabrics*.
Washington, DC: The Textile Museum, 1966
Graumont, Raoul and John Hensel *Square Knotting,
Tatting, Fringe and Needlework*. New York: Cornell
Maritime Press, 1946
Harvey, Virginia I. *Macramé, the Art of Creative Knotting*.
New York: Reinhold Publishing, 1967
Hersey, Jean *Wild Flowers to Know and Grow*. Princeton,
New Jersey: Van Nostrand Co. Inc., 1964
Dye Plants and Dyeing. New York: Brooklyn Botanic
Garden, 1964
Lyford, Carrie A. *Ojibwa (Chippewa) Crafts*. United States
Department of the Interior, Bureau of Indian Affairs,
Publications Service, Haskell Institute, Lawrence,
Kansas, 1943
Tattersall, C. E. C. *Notes on Carpet Knotting and Weaving*.
London: Victoria and Albert Museum, 1961
Tidball, Harriet *The Double Weave Plain and Patterned*.
Shuttle Craft Monograph One. Big Sur, California:
Craft and Hobby Book Service, 1960

Periodicals

Craft Horizons (American Craftsmen's Council Publication),
16 East 52nd Street, New York NY
Craftsman L'Artisan (Canadian Craftsmen's Association),
PO Box 2431, Station D, Ottawa, Canada
Handweaver and Craftsman, 220 Firth Avenue, New
York, NY

Index